BOEING 747

The first 10 years in service

JIM LUCAS

JANE'S
LONDON · NEW YORK · SYDNEY
AN AIRLINE PUBLICATIONS BOOK

First published in the United Kingdom in 1981 by
Jane's Publishing Company Limited
238 City Road, London EC1V 2PU

In co-operation with
Airline Publications and Sales Ltd
Noble Corner, Great West Road, Hounslow, Middx

ISBN 0 7106 0088 7

Computer Typesetting by Method Limited, Woodford Green, Essex
Printed in Great Britain by Hartnoll Print Limited, Bodmin, Cornwall

Contents

Dedication

To the Boeing people at Everett who build the mighty 747s and to the airline personnel who maintain and operate them – world-wide.

Acknowledgements

This book would not have been possible without the considerable assistance of The Boeing Company, and in particular Gordy Williams of Public Relations, Lonna Brooks the Photo Librarian, and the Photographic Department who created many of the superb illustrations.

Grateful thanks are also due to the Public Relations Departments of the engine manufacturers and the many airlines who contributed information and photographs.

Jim Lucas

247 to 747

After 10 years in service the Boeing 747 still retained an undisputed position as the world's largest airliner. By the end of 1979, with over 400 of these huge aircraft in service with more than 50 airlines, they could be seen, standing head and shoulders above the rest, at all major airports around the world. In the early years, with capacity to spare, they introduced the Spacious Age for long-distance air travellers, but, with the introduction of cheaper air fares in the late 1970s, they came into their own with their full capacity being utilised to bring the pleasure and benefits of world travel to millions more ordinary people.

Although Boeing originally gave the aircraft the name of Superjet, and almost everyone else referred to it by its nickname Jumbo Jet, it is now generally best known by its model number, 747. This model number was allocated in the established tradition of The Boeing Company to retain the lucky seven from each end of the model number of the well known 707, the company's first jet airliner, and simply change the centre figure; hence the 727, 737 and the forthcoming 757 and 767. The missing model number, 717, was allocated to the military version of the 707, the C-135 Stratolifter transport and KC-135 Stratotanker flight-refuelling tanker of the US Air Force.

The 707 was the first Boeing aircraft in a new 700 series, earlier aircraft having model numbers allocated generally in numerical order from the Model 1, the B & W two-seat biplane of 1916, to the Model 464, the B-52 Stratofortress. Model numbers in the 500 and 600 series were allocated to Boeing industrial products and missiles, respectively. Many of the earlier Boeing aircraft were better known by a name, such as Flying Fortress, Stratoliner, Superfortress, Stratofreighter, Stratocruiser and Stratojet or (where appropriate) their US Air Force designation B-17, B-29/B-50, C-97 and B-47, respectively. Outstanding exceptions were two famous Boeing civil aircraft of the 1930s, the Model 314 four-engined flying boat and the pioneering Model 247 twin-engined airliner.

Some well-known names in the foregoing list serve as a reminder that before Boeing became one of the world's major manufacturers of jet airliners the company was better known as a producer of big bombers for the US Air Force, both in World War II and in the Jet Age that followed. Also included in the list are the Boeing piston-engined airliners which made an important contribution during the various stages of development that have marked the progress of air travel over the past fifty years.

Boeing produced some single-engined and three-engined biplane airliners in the 1920s but it was in the early 1930s that the company made its first major contribution to air travel when it created the Model 247, the first of the 'modern' airliners. A low-wing monoplane of smooth, all-metal, stressed-skin construction with a streamlined fuselage, two cowled, radial engines mounted on the wings and a retractable landing gear, the Boeing 247 not only represented a technical revolution at the time but also set new standards for speed and passenger comfort.

This technical revolution did not occur overnight but started in 1930 when Boeing produced a single-engined mail carrier, the Monomail, which introduced the smooth, all-metal, low wing of clean, cantilever construction, and a retractable landing gear. The next stage was the company's experimental B-9 bomber, which was an all-metal, low-wing monoplane, with retractable landing gear, powered by two cowled, radial engines mounted on the wings; although not accepted for military service, it had a speed 5 m.p.h. faster than contemporary fighters and set a new standard for bombers in 1931.

The prototype of the Boeing 247, first of the 'modern' airliners. The lofty radio mast was shortened and repositioned on production aircraft. (Boeing)

The 247 airliner had a wing span of 74ft, a length of 51ft 4in and a gross weight of 12,650lb. Powered by two 550 h.p. Pratt & Whitney Wasp engines, it cruised at 155 m.p.h. and had a range of about 500 miles. The flight crew was two pilots.

Boeing Air Transport System (a subsidiary company, later to become United Air Lines) ordered 60 Boeing 247s off the drawing board, at a cost of $50,000 each, and introduced the first into service in May 1933. The aircraft's 5ft wide, soundproofed cabin provided accommodation for ten passengers, arranged in single seats at 40in pitch (providing ample knee room) down both sides of a central aisle, each with a large window. A toilet was provided at the rear of the cabin and a stewardess attended to passengers' needs. Boeing Air Transport had been the first to add a stewardess to the crew of its Boeing biplane airliners in 1930, to help the airsick passenger (quite common in those days of low-altitude flying) attend to the needs of women and children who may be travelling unaccompanied, serve coffee and sandwiches (or cold fried chicken lunches), and hand out chewing gum to passengers to clear their ears when it was time to land. The first eight women (all trained nurses) employed by the airline were remembered in 1975 by having their names painted on the nose of United Airlines' Boeing 747 N4712U *The Original Eight*. An unusual feature of the 247 was the passenger entrance door located on the right-hand side, but this was one change that did not become a new standard.

Competing with biplane airliners and thick-wing, corrugated-skinned Ford Tri-Motors then in general use, the 247 had no difficulty in proving its superior performance on US domestic routes, its 50 m.p.h. faster cruising speed reducing the journey time for the coast-to-coast New York to San Francisco service from 27hr to 19½hr, including seven stops en route.

Other airlines who tried to get in on the act and buy 247s for their own routes were unlucky because the production line was busy for a year producing the original order for 60 aircraft. One such airline, TWA (then known as Transcontinental and Western Air), looked elsewhere for an airliner capable of competing with the 247, and the result was the prototype DC-1, the first airliner from Douglas, and the production version, the DC-2, which entered service in July 1934. Following the basic twin-engined, all-metal monoplane formula of the 247, the DC-2 was slightly bigger (14 seats) with more powerful Wright Cyclone engines driving variable-pitch propellers, which gave it a higher cruising speed of 170 m.p.h., and had an additional improvement of being equipped with trailing-edge wing flaps.

The rest of the world was treated to a demonstration of these 'modern' airliners in October 1934 when a Boeing 247 (leased from United Air Lines and flown by Roscoe Turner and Clyde Pangborn) and a Douglas DC-2 (entered by KLM, Royal Dutch Airlines, and flown by Captain K.D. Parmentier and J.J. Moll) took part in the MacRobertson England to Australia air race over an 11,300-mile course from Mildenhall, Suffolk, to Melbourne. A specially-built de Havilland Comet racer won the race, but the airliners, with extra fuel tanks as their only special equipment, were not far behind it, the DC-2 coming second and the 247 third.

Another airliner to follow the Boeing 247 formula was the Lockheed L10 Electra, which entered service with Northwest Airlines in August 1934. Slightly smaller than the 247 and powered by two 400 h.p. Pratt & Whitney Wasp Junior engines, it incorporated the refinements of the DC-2 and started Lockheed's line of successful piston-engined airliners.

The airline business had suddenly taken off in the United States, and the intense competition between airlines, and between aircraft manufacturers struggling to meet their demands, resulted in the bigger and better airliners of later years. The engine manufacturers also played a vital part in this development because these 'modern' airliners required reliable engines with a good power-to-weight ratio. The Pratt & Whitney Wasp and the Wright Cyclone, both supercharged 9-cylinder, air-cooled radial engines, formed a good basis from which were developed two famous ranges of piston engines able to meet the demand for more power as aircraft grew in size. Powered by these engines, driving variable-pitch propellers, the all-metal, aerodynamically-refined airliners had the increased speed and reduced operating costs so necessary to make air travel a commercially viable proposition.

To compete with the DC-2, Boeing produced the improved 247D, which had variable-pitch propellers, Pratt & Whitney Wasp engines with reduction gearing and neater cowlings, an increased gross weight, a higher cruising speed and extended range, plus inflatable rubber 'boots' on the leading edges of the wings and tail for de-icing purposes. However, most airlines opted for the bigger DC-2 because of its better operating economics, and when American Airlines asked Douglas for a slightly bigger version, powered by 1000 h.p. engines, the result was the best-selling 21-seat DC-3.

Having set the standard for twin-engined airliners, Boeing was temporarily nudged out of the airliner business but this left the company free to pioneer the next stage of development – the four-engined, all-metal, low-wing monoplane. This appeared in the form of the B-17 Flying Fortress, the prototype of which made its first flight in July 1935; later, in its developed state, this became one of the famous bombers of World War II. As with the B-9, having proved the technical features of the basic B-17 design Boeing considered a civil version and mated the wings and tail of the bomber with an airliner fuselage to produce the Model 307 Stratoliner, the first of Boeing's high flyers – 'Strato' being an abbreviation of stratosphere.

Although not the first four-engined, all-metal, low-wing monoplane airliner, the Stratoliner was nevertheless a pioneer because it was the first airliner with a pressurised cabin to enter service. The pressurisation was only moderate, providing 8000ft conditions in the passenger cabin when the aircraft was cruising at 15,000ft, but it enabled the Stratoliner to fly above the worst of the rough weather, providing a smoother flight for its passengers, and the higher altitude improved its performance and gave it a better clearance over mountain ranges along the routes.

The Stratoliner had a wing span of 107ft 3in, a length of 74ft 4in and a gross weight of 42,000lb. Powered by four 1100 h.p. Wright Cyclone engines, it cruised at 220 m.p.h. and had a range of about 2000 miles. The flight crew was three, comprising two pilots and a flight engineer, and two stewardesses were carried.

TWA was first to put the Stratoliner into service, in July 1940, with an inaugural flight in both directions on its Super Sky Chief coast-to-coast service. The eastbound flight from Los Angeles to New York took 12¼hr and the westbound flight 14¼hr, both making only one stop, at Kansas City, en route. For technical reasons, the pressurised fuselage of the Stratoliner was of circular cross-section and its larger-than-usual diameter enabled passengers to be seated

The Stratoliner was the first airliner in service with a pressurised cabin. The unusual positioning of the cabin windows matched the seating arrangement. (TWA)

four abreast. For daytime flights, 33 passengers were carried in an unusual arrangement of nine single seats down the left-hand side of the cabin and four groups of facing triple seats down the right-hand side, with an offset aisle. This arrangement simplified the conversion for night-time flights when the nine passengers down the left-hand side had reclining seats and the four groups of seats on the right-hand side were converted into 16 berths, in groups of four (two curtained off double-tier berths) arranged laterally. This cabin arrangement resulted in the exterior of the aircraft having an odd appearance, with nine equally-spaced windows (plus one in the entrance door) on the left-hand side and eight windows arranged in spaced-out pairs on the right-hand side.

Only ten Stratoliners were built: a prototype, plus five for TWA, three for Pan American and one for the multi-millionaire Howard Hughes. Pan American introduced the Stratoliner on its Latin American routes out of Miami in September 1940 and had plans to use the aircraft on an experimental trans-Atlantic mail service between New York and London (Croydon) via Montreal, Moncton, Hattie's Camp (later Gander), Newfoundland, and Shannon, Eire. However, as with TWA, the aircraft had little time in airline service before the entry of the United States into World War II in December 1941, when the Stratoliners were transferred to military duties.

Pan American played a bigger part with the other Boeing airliner of this pre-war period: the Model 314 flying boat. Before Boeing started the design and

The Boeing 314 flying boat, operated by Pan American, was the first airliner to be used on commercial services across the Atlantic. (Boeing)

construction of the first B-17 it had been awarded a design study by the US Army Air Corps for an experimental long-range bomber which, when it made its first flight as the XB-15 in October 1937, was the largest and heaviest American aircraft built up to that time. It had a wing span of 149ft, a length of 87ft 7in, a gross weight of 70,706lb and a range of just over 5000 miles: the first of the 'modern' heavies. While the XB-15 was in the design stage in 1936, Pan American approached Boeing with a requirement for a long-range flying boat, and the result was the mating of the wings and tailplane of the XB-15 with a flying-boat hull to produce the ocean-going Model 314.

In the 1920s it was thought that airships were best suited for trans-ocean air travel because at the time they alone had the ability to carry a worthwhile number of fare-paying passengers, in addition to crew and fuel, non-stop over distances of thousands of miles. Britain and Germany devoted considerable effort to the development of civil airships; these were aptly named, being aviation's equivalent of ocean liners and providing spacious accommodation for their passengers, who slept in cabins and had the use of public rooms such as a lounge, dining room and bar. This high level of passenger comfort was necessary, however, because journey times for trans-Atlantic flights could be counted in days rather than hours.

Although the British R100 made one trial trans-Atlantic flight to Canada and back in July 1930, the Imperial Airship Scheme never got to the stage of carrying fare-paying passengers because all plans were dropped with the loss of the R101 on its way to India in October 1930. However, the Germans were more successful with their *Graf Zeppelin*, which was launched in 1928 and was used on a passenger service across the South Atlantic to Rio de Janeiro from 1931 to 1937. The early success of this operation led to the building of the larger *Hindenburg*, which in May 1936 started the first regular air service across the North Atlantic for the carriage of passengers, cargo and mail. If the Boeing 707 is today considered big, and the 747 huge, then the *Hindenburg* was vast. It was 803ft long and 135ft in diameter, and was powered by four 1320 h.p. diesel engines which gave it a cruising speed of 78 m.p.h. and an endurance of 109hr or a range of over 8000 miles in still air; the crew totalled 55 who worked in watches (shifts) naval style. Accommodation was provided for 50 passengers who paid a fare of $400 single or $720 return, sharing a two-berth cabin, for the flight between Frankfurt and Lakehurst, New Jersey, which took on average 65hr westbound and 52hr eastbound. The service was operated during summer only, and during the 1936 season ten scheduled round trips were operated, which indicated its closer association to an ocean-liner sailing schedule than an airline timetable. For the 1937 season 18-round trips had been planned but on the first of these, in May 1937, the *Hindenburg* caught fire at Lakehurst and ended not only the German airship operations but also the golden age of civil airships.

Flying boats were next to enjoy their golden age on long-distance air routes. These aircraft had been developed from the early machines built by Glenn Curtiss in America before World War I, through the wood and fabric biplane and braced metal monoplane stages to the 'modern' all-metal, stressed-skin, cantilever monoplanes of the mid-1930s, but unlike the 'modern' landplanes of the time they were high-wing monoplanes to keep their engines clear of the water. The four-engined Short C Class (Empire) flying boats were the first of these, and Imperial Airways ordered 28 for service from October 1936 onwards on its routes to Egypt, East and South Africa, India, Malaya and Australia. Flying boats were chosen for these mainly overland routes because of the poor facilities that existed at the time for landplanes, the flying boats being able to operate from sheltered harbours, rivers and inland lakes.

Another application for civil flying boats was on trans-ocean routes where, in the 1930s, it was thought that if a forced landing should become necessary there would be a better chance of survival in a flying boat than in a landplane. This 'psychological safety' aspect applied particularly to the passengers of this pioneering period who were comforted by the rugged appearance of a big flying boat.

Pan American comes into the story here because, after developing an extensive route network in Latin America during the late 1920s and early 1930s, its president, Juan Trippe, set his sights on conquering the oceans on each side of the United States. The Pacific came first because of its less severe weather conditions and its less complicated landing-rights situation, the mid-

Pacific islands of Hawaii, Midway, Wake, Guam and the Philippines all being US territories. Survey flights were started in April 1935 using a four-engined Sikorsky S-42 stripped of its passenger accommodation and equipped with extra fuel tanks to enable it to fly non-stop the 2400 miles between San Francisco and Honolulu, Hawaii. The first scheduled air-mail flight across the Pacific was made in November 1935 using the bigger and more capable four-engined Martin M-130, and three of these aircraft were available for the start of a weekly scheduled passenger service from San Francisco to Manila in the Philippines which was inaugurated in October 1936 (with an extension to Hong Kong in April 1937). Although capable of carrying 32 passengers on the shorter sectors of the route, the M-130 could carry only 12 to 15 passengers on the long sector between San Francisco and Honolulu, but in those days passengers were not all that numerous and mail carrying contributed a great deal to an airline's revenue.

The North Atlantic took a little more time and effort to conquer because of its strong prevailing westerly winds, often with bad weather and severe icing conditions (particularly in winter), and also because most pieces of land around it belonged to a different country. Two routes between the USA and Britain or France were planned, the more direct northern route via Shediac (New Brunswick, Canada), Botwood (Newfoundland) and Foynes (Eire), which would be suitable only for summer services, and a southern route via Bermuda, the Azores and Lisbon. Survey flights and experimental mail-carrying flights were carried out from 1937 onwards by Imperial Airways and Pan American, using Short C Class and Sikorsky S-42 flying boats, respectively, but passenger services had to await the delivery of a bigger and better flying boat: the Boeing 314, the 'jumbo' of the golden age of civil flying boats.

When delivered in 1939, the Boeing 314 was the largest and most advanced aircraft produced up to that time in the United States. It had a wing span of 152ft, a length of 106ft and a gross weight of 82,500lb. Powered by four 14-cylinder, 1500 h.p. Wright Double Cyclone engines (the most powerful engines to be fitted to a pre World War II airliner), it cruised at 180 m.p.h. and had a range of about 3000 miles. The flight crew was seven, comprising captain, first officer, navigator, engineer, radio officer and junior flight officer, plus reserve crew members (with crew rest area) for long flights, who were all located on an upper deck.

The deep hull could accommodate up to 74 passengers on short sectors but for long trans-ocean flights this was reduced to 35 passengers, who enjoyed accommodation and facilities almost equal to airship passengers. Although not having quite the number of public rooms as an airship, the 314 did have a separate dining room, and the passengers sat or slept (in berths) in five separate compartments on the main deck, and there was also a promenade area and a self-contained suite in the rear. Forward on the main deck was a big galley in which two stewards prepared hot meals.

Six of these large flying boats were ordered initially by Pan American at a cost of $550,000 each, with deliveries at monthly intervals from January 1939. The first two were allocated to the trans-Pacific route and the remaining four to the trans-Atlantic route. After a survey flight to Southampton via the southern route in March 1939, a mail flight to Marseilles was operated on the route on May 20, 1939, the 12th anniversary of Charles Lindbergh's famous solo flight from New York to Paris. This was followed by passenger flights on both the southern route to Marseilles and the northern route to Southampton carrying invited guests of Pan American. Then on June 28, 1939 Pan American's 314 *Dixie Clipper* operated the first fare-paying passenger service by flying boat on the southern route to Marseilles, and on July 8, 1939 the airline's 314 *Yankee Clipper* operated the first fare-paying passenger service by flying boat on the northern route to Southampton.

According to Bradshaw's Air Guide for August 1939, a weekly service was being operated on both the northern and southern routes, and the fare quoted was $375 one-way and $675 return. For the northern route, departure from Port Washington, New York, was at 0730 hours on Saturdays with a 1hr stop at Shediac and a 1½hr stop at Botwood before departing at 1800 on the overnight, 2000 mile over-ocean sector to Foynes; arrival there was due at 0830 next morning and, after a 1hr stop, arrival at Southampton was scheduled for 1300 (a train then took passengers from Southampton Docks to London). The return service left Southampton at 1400 on Wednesdays and, after a 1hr stop, departed Foynes at 1630 for the overnight ocean crossing, arriving at Botwood at 0530 next morning; after a 1½hr stop there and a 1hr stop at Shediac, the arrival at Port Washington was scheduled for 1400. The southern route to Marseilles was operated with a night stop in Lisbon which lengthened the journey time somewhat but this was probably done to avoid passengers having to spend two nights in succession aboard the aircraft, the first night outbound (or second night inbound) being spent on the 2,375 mile over-ocean sector between Port Washington and the Azores (or vice versa), which was flown non-stop, missing out Bermuda. Total distances for the two routes were given as 3,411 miles for New York – Southampton and 4,251 miles for New York – Marseilles. The northern route was planned to be operated in summer only, so the New York – Southampton figure for winter months would have been considerably greater.

Like the airships, flying boats were a breed apart from the landplane mainstream and both borrowed a lot from the nautical fraternity. Juan Trippe is said to have considered Pan American ocean-going, four-engined flying boats as modern equivalents of the clippers (wind-driven sailing ships) which had plied the world's trade routes in earlier times, hence the aircraft got clipper names; a tradition continued to this day on the airline's Boeing 747s. He is also credited with introducing a standard uniform for flight crews and with giving them their titles of Captain, First Officer, etc. Regardless of these frills, under Juan Trippe's leadership, Pan American led the way with its flying boats on the world's major trans-ocean air routes.

Regrettably, the golden age of the civil flying boat over the North Atlantic was cut short by the outbreak of World War II in Europe in September 1939. This led to the closure of the northern route and the curtailment of the southern route at Lisbon, and the eventual transfer to military requirements. Civil operations continued on the trans-Pacific route until the Japanese attack on

Pearl Harbour, Hawaii, in December 1941, when these too became a military operation.

During the summer of 1939 Pan American ordered a further six Boeing 314s with improved range and performance. Designated 314A, these had increased fuel capacity, an increased gross weight of 84,000lb, and were powered by 1600 h.p. Wright Double Cyclone engines. The war had started in Europe before these were delivered and three of them were diverted to British Overseas Airways Corporation (BOAC), as Imperial Airways had become. The earlier aircraft were later modified to this standard.

Although flying boats played an important part in World War II, across the Atlantic and Pacific, and elsewhere, the tide of progress was flowing against them and during the six war years the faster and more economical landplane achieved a state of development where it could take over the trans-ocean routes. Over the North Atlantic during the early war years, military necessity required risks to be taken for the delivery of bombers by air to avoid heavy losses by U-boat sinkings when deliveries were made by surface ships. These risks would have been unacceptable for a civil operation but they resulted in the North Atlantic winter being conquered by the rapid development of meteorological and air traffic control services plus improvements in aircraft de-icing, navigation and communication equipment. Initially the flights were mainly eastbound but eventually westbound flights had to be made in winter as well as summer to provide a quicker return of the ferry crews. The bigger landplane bombers and transports necessitated the building of properly equipped bases with concrete runways on both sides of the Atlantic (such as at Gander in Newfoundland and Prestwick in Scotland) and throughout the various war zones as the battle spread.

The far-flung war zones created a supply problem and large numbers of transport aircraft were built to meet this need. The four-engined Douglas DC-4 and Lockheed Constellation, both of the 'modern' standard with the additional improvement of a nosewheel landing gear, were already in the early production stage when the United States entered the war in December 1941 so the first aircraft came off the production lines in camouflage instead of airline colours to serve on the long-range routes.

When peace returned to the North Atlantic in 1945 it was some time before full civil passenger services were re-started, having to await aircraft deliveries and the preparation of overseas bases, but when they did the situation was very different from that which had existed for those few months of operations just prior to the war. The US Civil Aeronautics Board had decided to allow competition on international routes, so these were no longer Pan American's alone, and the chosen airlines all opted for the four-engined landplane, initially in the form of the war-surplus, unpressurised DC-4s and later the new and improved Constellations and DC-6s (both pressurised) as production lines changed over to civil airliners again.

The first airline to start a scheduled passenger service with landplanes over the North Atlantic was a newcomer, American Overseas Airlines (AOA, a subsidiary of American Airlines), who operated a DC-4 from New York (La

Guardia) to London via Gander and Shannon, Eire, on October 23, 1945; the London terminal was initially Hurn Airport, near Bournemouth, until London Airport (Heathrow) was ready. Next came Pan American, also with a DC-4 on the New York – London route, replacing the Boeing 314 flying boats used for a few post-war months, and then came the other newcomer to civil international services, TWA, operating a DC-4 from New York to Paris; the aircraft carried the new title Trans World Airline (singular): the company's name was not changed to Trans World Airlines until 1950.

By the time the first post-war issue of Bradshaw's Air Guide was published in May 1946 the North Atlantic route was showing the beginnings of the major air route it was to become. AOA was operating a daily service to London, mostly from New York, with one via Boston and one originating at Washington, plus a weekly service from Chicago and a weekly service from Washington and Philadelphia. The airline was also operating a weekly service from New York to Copenhagen, Oslo and Stockholm, and a weekly service from New York to Amsterdam. Pan American was operating a daily New York – London service, and three services a week from New York to Lisbon, with two of these flights continuing on to Dakar and Monrovia (it had also re-started its trans-Pacific flights with a daily service between San Francisco and Honolulu). TWA was operating a daily service between New York and Paris, with one a week continuing on to Geneva, plus three additional services which originated at either Chicago or Washington and Philadelphia, and called at Rome, Athens and Cairo or Madrid, Lisbon, Rome and Cairo. All trans-Atlantic flights by the three US airlines were via Gander and Shannon, and the New York – London and New York – Paris fares were started at the pre-war price of $375 single or $675 return.

BOAC operated its Boeing 314 flying boats on the southern route during the winter of 1945/46 but did not start London – New York landplane services until July 1946. KLM, Royal Dutch Airlines, started Amsterdam – New York services towards the end of May, Air France started Paris – New York services in June, and the 1946 list of trans-Atlantic operators was completed in September when SILA, Swedish Intercontinental Airlines (later to become part of Scandinavian Airlines System, SAS), started a service from Stockholm to New York via Prestwick.

The DC-4s, DC-6s and Constellations plying the North Atlantic route were joined in 1949 by a new Boeing airliner – the Stratocruiser – for a share of what was to become the golden age of the long-range, piston-engined airliner. Boeing spent the war years mass-producing bombers, having the B-17 Flying Fortress in production at the beginning, and ending the war, in more ways than one, with the B-29 Superfortress, the atomic-bomb dropper. A military transport had been designed during the war, based on the wings and tail of the B-29, but production of this, the Model 367, or C-97 Stratofreighter as it became known, did not start until the war was over when it came into its own serving mainly as a flight-refuelling tanker (KC-97), and 888 were built.

An airliner counterpart of the C-97, the Stratocruiser was another big one from Boeing. It had a wing span of 141ft 3in, a length of 110ft 4in and a gross

The Stratocruiser – Boeing's big piston-engined airliner of the 1950s. The windows of the downstairs lounge are visible behind the wing. (Boeing)

weight of 145,000lb. Power was provided by four of the most powerful piston engines ever made, the 3500 h.p. Pratt & Whitney Wasp Major, which had 28 cylinders arranged radially in four banks of seven, an arrangement that earned it the nickname of Corncob. These engines gave the Stratocruiser a cruising speed of 300 m.p.h. at an altitude of 25,000ft and its range was about 3000 miles. The flight crew for trans-Atlantic services was five, comprising captain, first officer, navigator, flight engineer and radio officer.

Only 56 Stratocruisers were built and they were sold, at a cost of $1.5 million each, initially to five airlines: Pan American 21, American Overseas Airlines 8, Northwest Airlines 10, BOAC 10 and United Air Lines 7.

The Stratocruiser entered service at a time when competition between trans-Atlantic airlines was hotting up. In the early post-war years there was only one fare (equivalent to today's first-class fare) and the passengers of the time, film stars, politicians, businessmen and the otherwise wealthy, were offered a variety of 'extras' by the airlines vying for their custom. The Stratocruiser was ideally suited to this situation, having a spacious and comfortable interior which is best described as the landplane equivalent of the big flying boats. The passenger cabin was wider than those of the DC-6 and Constellation, allowing ample elbow room with the normal four-abreast seating (pairs of seats on each side of a central aisle), and the interior was divided into three compartments separated by dressing rooms/toilets forward and a galley towards the rear. In addition, there was a lower-deck lounge, just behind the wing and reached by a spiral staircase from the main deck, which was equipped with 14 seats and a bar; this lounge was very popular with passengers, giving them the opportunity to stretch their legs and have a change of scene to break the monotony of long flights, there being no in-flight entertainment at the time.

A trans-Atlantic flight from London to New York in the early 1950s took about 17hr with one stop but this was only possible when the weather was favourable, otherwise another refuelling stop was necessary; eastbound flights could sometimes be made non-stop but usually required one stop. Most flights were made overnight, and berths were available in the two forward compartments of a Stratocruiser at extra cost. The normal accommodation for daytime flights was for 60 passengers but this was reduced for night-time flights according to the number of berths required in the forward compartments. The ultimate in Stratocruiser trans-Atlantic flights was reached with Pan American's *President* and BOAC's *Monarch* luxury services, in which, for a surcharge of $50, passengers were really given the 'treatment', including a seven-course dinner with champagne and a berth for the night. Cabin staff on these services comprised four stewards and a stewardess, with one steward permanently on duty in the lower-deck bar.

Such luxury was, of course, available for only a few, but two events in May 1952 marked the beginning of a major change in air travel. The first of these was the introduction by the trans-Atlantic airlines of 'second class' (but given the name of tourist class), and the second event was the introduction by BOAC of the world's first jet airliner service. In a few years the results of these events would culminate in economy-class travel aboard long-range jet airliners, opening up the airways to millions of people.

Reduced fares had been tried earlier on a limited scale, particularly on US domestic routes (where it was known as 'coach class'), and Pan American introduced tourist-class services on its New York – San Juan (Puerto Rico) route in 1948; the success of these services led Juan Trippe, Pan American's president who had long advocated the provision of safe, comfortable air travel at the lowest possible cost, to press for the introduction of tourist class on the trans-Atlantic route. It took some time for this to be achieved because of the number of governments involved but eventually the airlines of IATA (International Air Transport Association) reached agreement to introduce a tourist class with a fare for New York to London of $270 single, compared with $395 single first class. Pan American was first to operate a trans-Atlantic tourist class service with a DC-6B between New York and London on May 1, 1952. Separate aircraft were used for the two classes, and to get the same revenue from a tourist-class aircraft an additional line of seats was added to the cabin, making it five abreast instead of four abreast (reducing elbow room) but still retaining the 40in seat pitch (for ample leg room), and the cabin service was reduced to meals and beverages, with alcoholic drinks having to be purchased. Pan American DC-6Bs carried 82 passengers when arranged for tourist class or 52 with a first-class layout, and in BOAC L049 Constellations the figures were 68 and 43, respectively.

Passenger carrying on the North Atlantic route now boomed, and the line on the IATA airlines' graph soared from the 342,000-a-year mark in 1951 to the 1 million-a-year mark in 1957. That was the year when the number of trans-Atlantic air travellers equalled the number of trans-Atlantic sea travellers. Thereafter the line on the graph for the ocean liners began to drop while the line for the airliners climbed on to even greater heights. One of the major reasons for this was yet another fare cut: this time the introduction of economy fares in 1958. At first these were introduced as a 'third class', offering a cheaper fare for a further lowering of comfort standards, but after a few years 'economy' displaced 'tourist' and became the standard for second class. When economy fares were first introduced, the New York to London single fares were $435 first class, $315 tourist class and $252 economy class.

Whereas tourist class reduced elbow room but kept the seat rows at 40in pitch and in line with the windows, economy class took the reductions a stage further and added extra passengers by also reducing the seat pitch to 34in, thereby reducing leg room and putting all seat rows out of alignment with the windows in aircraft designed for a first-class layout. However, this further reduction in comfort had to be endured for less time because in 1958 the first jet airliners were introduced on the North Atlantic route, which cut journey times.

Trans-Atlantic journey times had been reduced to about 12hr in 1956/57 with the introduction of the ultimate in long-range, piston-engined airliners, the DC-7C and L1649 Starliner, which were capable of making non-stop flights in both directions, winter and summer. The higher cruising speeds of the first jet airliners on the route cut this time even further.

The jet airliner was a long time coming to the North Atlantic because in the early post-war years the fuel-guzzling jet engines of the time were suitable only for either short-duration fighters or bombers supported by flight-refuelling tankers, certainly not for long-range airliners. However, rapid development of the jet engine for military purposes soon made it suitable for short-to-medium-range airliners, and the de Havilland Comet 1 introduced by BOAC on a stopping service from London to Johannesburg on May 2, 1952 demonstrated to the world the pleasures of smooth, fast travel by jet airliner. This initial version carried only 36 passengers in a spacious first-class arrangement, but the bigger, extended-range Comet 3 was in the early production state to meet a Pan American order for a trans-Atlantic version when the Comet 1 ran into trouble in 1954 and the type had to be withdrawn from service. Trans-Atlantic passengers then had to wait a further four years for their first taste of jet travel.

Meanwhile, Boeing had continued to build bombers for the US Air Force, producing its first jet-powered type, the six-engined B-47 Stratojet, in 1947, and following this with the bigger eight-engined B-52 Stratofortress in 1952. Both designs had swept-back wings with their jet engines in 'pods' mounted on pylons beneath the wings, an arrangement which set the pattern for many future designs. With the increasing number of jet-powered fighters and bombers entering service, there appeared to be a requirement for a jet-powered flight-refuelling tanker to support them, and therefore Boeing set to work designing one based on the earlier Model 367 KC-97. Early designs featured a

KC-97 double-bubble fuselage with swept-back wings powered by four jet engines mounted in pairs on each wing, but eventually the Model 367-80 (the 80th variant of the Model 367) emerged with a sleek fuselage and a swept-back wing equipped with four engines in separate pods. Boeing put its own money into this project and the company's management gave the go-ahead to build a prototype in August 1952.

Like the C-97, the new design had possibilities as an airliner as well as a transport/tanker, and when Dash Eighty (-80) made its first flight on July 15, 1954 it had the almost windowless fuselage of a military tanker but carried a civilian registration N70700, and the aircraft served as a prototype for both the KC-135 Stratotanker and the Model 707 airliner. The military version was the first to be ordered, in October 1954, and 820 were eventually produced. The airlines at the time were content with their fleets of piston-engined airliners so were in no hurry to make the change to jet airliners, considering them to be too big and to have doubtful operating economics. Then, in October 1955, Pan American took the bold step and ordered 20 Boeing 707s at a cost of just over $4 million each, plus 25 Douglas DC-8s, the first of which was not due to fly until May 1958 but appeared to offer better range. Most of the trans-Atlantic airlines, and others, soon followed Pan American's lead and ordered jet airliners. And Boeing was back in the airliner business – this time to stay.

Jet Clipper Liberty Bell, a Boeing 707-321 of Pan American, one of the long-range big-jets of the 1960s. (Pan American)

Production of the 707 started with the 120 Series, a domestic version intended for non-stop coast-to-coast services. It had a wing span of 130ft 10in, a length of 145ft 1in, and a gross weight of 248,000lb. Power was provided by four Pratt & Whitney JT3C turbo-jets, each giving 13,500lb of thrust. It cruised at between 550 and 600 m.p.h. at 30,000 to 35,000ft, and it had a range of about 3000 miles.

BOAC was first to introduce jet airliners on the trans-Atlantic route when it started de Havilland Comet 4 services between London and New York on October 4, 1958. Pan American followed soon after with its first service with a Boeing 707-120 from New York to Paris on October 26, 1958. These early services were of an interim nature, requiring one refuelling stop on the way, but the higher cruising speed of these jet airliners reduced the westbound journey time to around 9½hr and the services paved the way for the eventual non-stop operations of the extended-range 707-320 (Pratt & Whitney powered) and 707-420 (Rolls-Royce powered) which took over the route in October 1959 (Pan American) and May 1960 (BOAC), respectively.

The 707-320 Intercontinental was the main production version. It had a wing span of 142ft 5in, a length of 152ft 11in and a gross weight of 316,000lb. Power was provided by four 15,800lb thrust Pratt & Whitney JT4A turbo-jets which gave it a cruising speed of between 550 and 600 m.p.h. at 30,000 to 35,000ft and its range was just over 4000 miles. The 707-420 was similar but was powered by four 17,500lb thrust Rolls-Royce Conway by-pass engines (an early version of the turbo-fan). The later production versions, the 707-320B and 707-320C, were powered by four 18,000lb thrust Pratt & Whitney JT3D turbo-fans and had an increased wing span of 145ft 9in, a higher gross weight of 336,000lb and an increased range (707-320B) of 6,000 miles. The flight crew on trans-Atlantic services was four, comprising captain, first officer, flight engineer and navigator.

Because the 707 was introduced at a time of tourist/economy class, the passenger cabin was designed to suit the new way of life, with a row of small, closely-spaced windows down each side, ensuring that every economy-class seat row was adjacent to at least one window, and a cabin width to accept six-abreast seating (a triple seat on each side of a central aisle). In general, the aircraft were operated in a mixed-class configuration from the start with, typically, a small first-class compartment (seating around 20 passengers arranged four abreast at 40in pitch) forward, and a large economy-class compartment (seating around 125 passengers arranged six abreast at 34in pitch) at the rear. The usual cabin crew was five, who, depending on the airline, could be stewardesses or stewards or a mixture of both.

With the combination of economy class fares and the popularity of the big-jets, the Boeing 707 and Douglas DC-8, joined in 1965 by the British Super VC10, the line on the IATA airlines' trans-Atlantic passenger-carrying graph soared on to even greater heights. In 1967, ten years after the 1 million mark had been passed, the line passed the 5.5 million passengers-a-year mark, and was still climbing. The non-stop flights had reduced the journey time between Europe and America to about 8hr, and the time passed easier with the help of in-flight movies first introduced by TWA in 1961 and quickly followed by most other airlines.

By the mid-1960s the so-called big-jets were showing signs of not being big enough. The forecast for the growth of air traffic indicated a 12 per cent annual increase and to meet future demand a bigger aircraft would be required on long-range routes instead of continuing to add to the number of existing aircraft, which would lead to congestion of airways and airports. Both Boeing and Douglas worked on plans to enlarge their existing aircraft, and Douglas was first to introduce a 250-seat version of its DC-8 which met immediate requirements. The design of the 707 did not lend itself to a simple 'stretching' operation and therefore Boeing took the major step and went for the really big one.

Earlier, the major US aircraft manufacturers, Boeing, Douglas and Lockheed, had been invited to participate in a US Air Force design competition for a very large transport aircraft which would be twice the size of existing transports and would be equipped with engines giving twice the power of the then current turbo-fans. This competition gave the aircraft and engine manufacturers the incentive to think big and evolve technology to meet the new challenge. Lockheed eventually won the competition with its C-5A Galaxy powered by General Electric big-fan engines, but that turned out to be a good day for long-distance air travellers because all the effort expended by Boeing designers and engineers on the military transport project was then utilised in the design of a very large airliner, the mighty Boeing 747.

The military transport had required a high wing so that the main deck in the fuselage could be at a low level to simplify the loading of tanks and other large vehicles, but the initial designs of the 747 featured a mid-wing and a double-deck fuselage with a width not much greater than that of the 707. However, airline reaction was not favourable towards a two-deck arrangement from an emergency-evacuation viewpoint, and the design was finalised around a low-wing aircraft with a single main deck much wider than that of the 707 – 20ft wide providing for up to ten-abreast seating, arranged three, four, three, with two aisles – the first of the wide-bodied airliners. In this arrangement, up to 500 passengers could be carried in a high-density layout (ten-abreast, all economy class) and the lower part of the fuselage provided large holds for cargo as well as the usual baggage and mail. To meet the requirement for a freighter version, the flight deck was located on a level above the main deck so that the nose of the fuselage could be hinged upwards to provide easy access to the main deck; the 20ft fuselage width also fitted in with this requirement, allowing two 8ft-wide containers to be accommodated side-by-side along the main length of the fuselage. Fairing the flight deck into the top of the fuselage, to give the 747 its distinctive hump on top, left a compartment behind it which Boeing advertised as an upstairs lounge in the passenger-carrying versions and linked it to the main deck by a spiral staircase, similar to that of the Stratocruiser.

With such a wide fuselage, the other dimensions of the 747 had to be equally impressive. It was to have a wing span of 195ft 8in, a length of 231ft 4in and a gross weight of 680,000lb. Power was to be provided by four 41,000lb thrust

Models showing the evolution of the 747 design from double-deck varieties to the final version in the centre of the front row.

(Boeing)

Pratt & Whitney JT9D-1 big-fan engines which would give the aircraft a cruising speed of 600 m.p.h. at an altitude of 30,000 – 40,000ft and it would have a range to match that of the contemporary long-range jet airliners which could fly non-stop from Europe to the US west coast.

In March 1966, Boeing decided to proceed with the 747 programme on a tentative basis, and the following month Pan American placed its incredible order for 25 of these huge airliners at a cost of $20 million each. In announcing the order, Juan Trippe said that the lower operating costs of the 747s could lead to further cuts in fares. As with the airline's pioneering order for 707s eleven years earlier, other airlines soon followed Pan American's lead. In July 1966, William M. Allen, president of Boeing, confirmed that the board of the company had decided to go ahead with the development and production of the 747.

A Boeing advertisement which appeared at the time of the go-ahead described the 747 as "Ushering in a new era in jet transportation. For passengers – an entirely new concept in air travel comfort and spaciousness. For airlines – the fastest, quietest, most profitable airliner in commercial aviation history".

Under Construction

Following the go-ahead, Boeing was faced with the gigantic task of not only building the world's largest airliner but also producing sufficient 747s in a short period to satisfy the demand from the numerous airlines (particularly those on the trans-Atlantic route) who could see the competitive threat of the order from pacemaking Pan American and had to order some 747s of their own. By the end of 1966 the orders stood at 88 from 11 airlines, and the mighty airliner was still at the drawing-board stage. Programme target dates were: late 1968 for completion of the first aircraft; September 1969 for first deliveries; and December 1972 for delivery of the 200th aircraft.

During the following three years there was intense activity in the State of Washington, located in the north-west corner of the United States. This had been the home of The Boeing Company since 1916 when William Edward Boeing started building biplanes at Seattle. Expansion of facilities through the ensuing years included an additional factory at nearby Renton and another at Wichita in Kansas, but with these extensive facilities busy producing 707s, 727s and 737s a new factory had to be built to mass produce the huge 747. The site chosen was close to the city of Everett, nearly 30 miles north of Seattle and alongside Snohomish County Airport, which is usually referred to by its earlier US Air Force name of Paine Field. Preparation of the 780-acre site began in June 1966 and the construction of the buildings started in the late summer of that year.

To assemble the world's largest airliners Boeing had to build the world's largest building (in terms of volume), a structure containing approximately 200 million cubic feet and covering about 43 acres. This main building is divided into three vast bays, each 1000ft long, 300ft wide and 115ft high. One bay houses the sub-assembly areas for the wings and sections of the fuselage, and the other two bays each house a final assembly line with stations for four complete aircraft and an area at the start of the line for wings-to-centre section (wing stub) joining and wings-to-centre fuselage mating. The bays are linked and served by eleven 30-ton-capacity overhead cranes which transfer the sub-assemblies through various stages of build-up and eventually carry the completed sub-assemblies to the start of one of the final assembly lines.

The first Boeing manufacturing personnel began work at the $200 million Everett factory in January 1967, and the buildings were occupied in stages throughout the year as each was completed. The main assembly building became activated in May 1967, only a year after the start of the programme, and the actual assembly of components into sub-assemblies for the first 747 began in September of that year.

Although Boeing designers had considerable experience with big jet aircraft, like the B-52 and 707, they still had problems with this project, their biggest yet.

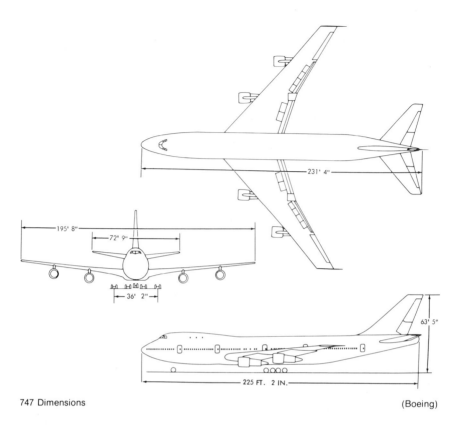

747 Dimensions

(Boeing)

Their main problem was the unexpected increases in the weights of the structure and systems which caused the gross weight of the aircraft to go way above the planned 680,000lb. A severe weight-reduction programme was conducted in all areas and eventually the gross weight was held at 710,000lb. However, this increase meant that more power would be required from the engines if the 747 was to meet its promised performance specifications and therefore Pratt & Whitney was called on to condense the JT9D development programme and make available the more powerful JT9D-3 of 43,500lb thrust for the first production aircraft.

One of the features of the 747 programme is that it has one of the largest sub-contracting arrangements in the history of commercial aircraft manufacturing. With no government funds for this programme, which was estimated to require an investment of $1 billion by the time the first 747s were delivered, Boeing arranged a work and cost/profit sharing agreement with some other American aircraft manufacturers. In this way, Northrop make the components for the main fuselage sections at Hawthorne, California, and send them by rail to Everett for assembly, a spur from the local railway line actually extending into the end of the main assembly building so that the components are unloaded inside it. Vought Systems Division of LTV (formerly Ling-Temco-Vought) make the rear fuselage, tailplane (horizontal stabiliser) and fin and rudder at Dallas, Texas; Rockwell International (formerly North American Rockwell) build the lower section of the centre fuselage and the fixed leading-edge of the wings at Tulsa, Oklahoma; Fairchild Republic (formerly Fairchild Hiller) make the leading-edge and trailing-edge wing flaps, and the ailerons and spoilers, at Farmingdale, New York; Rhor Industries build the engine pods and pylons at Chula Vista, California; and Aeronca makes the flap-track ('canoe') fairings at Middletown, Ohio, and its Aerocal Division makes wing-box ribs at Torrance, California. In addition, the twin-wheel nose landing gear and the four-leg, 16-wheel main landing gear is supplied by Cleveland Pneumatic of Cleveland, Ohio; the cargo handling systems in the under-floor cargo holds are supplied by Western Gear Corporation of Everett; and the Pratt & Whitney engines come from East Hartford, Connecticut.

These companies are the major sub-contractors in the 747 programme, but there are also approximately 1500 primary suppliers and some 15,000 secondary suppliers located in most of the states of the USA and eight foreign countries. In fact, more than half of each 747 by weight and dollar value is sub-contracted to outside firms. These sub-contracted items are made to Boeing's engineering specifications and quality standards, and are delivered to Everett by rail, road or air for assembly into complete aircraft.

Around $4\frac{1}{2}$ million parts (including small items like fasteners) are required to make one 747, and, with many of the big items coming from all over the country, the major task is getting them all together at the right time at Everett, so the entire operation is monitored by computer. It takes approximately 21 months to build a 747 from scratch, but only the last two months of this time are spent on the final assembly line. Much of the component and system installation work is done at the sub-assembly stage so that major sub-assemblies are almost complete by the time they are brought together on the final assembly line.

Apart from the assembly of the major sub-assemblies from components made elsewhere, and the final assembly of the complete aircraft, Boeing's share of the 747 programme includes the manufacture of components for the main structural part of the wing, the wing box, and the nose section of the fuselage. Another new factory was built at Auburn (about 20 miles south of Seattle) to serve as a machine shop and fabricating plant for the Boeing part of the programme. Among the components manufactured there are the huge panels which go to make up the top and bottom of the wing box. These panels are machined from solid billets of aluminium, the largest being over 100ft long, 5ft wide and 1in thick. Numerical-tape-controlled milling machines remove the unwanted metal, whittling away over two-thirds of it, to produce a tapered and shaped panel. These, together with other lengthy items like spars and stringers, are delivered to Everett on special road vehicles. Auburn also made many of the specialised machines, precision tools and assembly jigs for the programme, including the massive wing-assembly jigs for use at Everett. The structural components for the nose section of the 747s are made at Boeing's factory at Wichita, Kansas, and are delivered by rail to Everett.

The start of the final assembly line where the wings are joined and the centre body is attached to the wing assembly   (Boeing)

The components for the nose section of the first 747, comprising frames, stringers and skin panels, arrived at Everett towards the end of 1967 and went into assembly jigs which had been made earlier at Wichita. These components were then riveted together to form the nose sub-assembly (referred to in the factory as Section 41). The components for the 20ft diameter main fuselage, made by Northrop, are assembled in jigs in a similar manner, but for ease of handling are built initially in 'small' sub-assemblies: Section 42, between the nose and the wing; Section 44: the centre section over the wing; Section 46: between the wing and the tail; and Section 48: the tail section. Before being taken by overhead crane to one of the final assembly lines, Sections 41 and 42 are bolted together to form the forward body, and Sections 46 and 48 are bolted together to form the aft body.

Left-hand and right-hand wing boxes are built up separately, from the machined panels, spars, ribs and stringers, in assembly jigs located in the sub-assembly bay of the main assembly building. When completed each of these is 120ft long, with a width of nearly 20ft and a thickness of 7ft at its root end, and weighs 28,000lb. After assembly, the wing boxes are removed from the jigs by overhead crane for transfer to a clean, seal and paint shop, which is an extension of the main assembly building. Here, the interior of the wing boxes are washed out and sealed to form the integral fuel tanks; there are three tanks in each wing box which, together with a tank formed in the centre section (wing stub), provided early aircraft with a total capacity of US47,210gal of fuel. The exterior of the wing boxes, which are machined surfaces, are also painted here to protect them from corrosion. The wing boxes are then returned to the assembly bay to have the leading-edge and trailing-edge fixed structure added before being transferred to the start of one of the final assembly lines where the left-hand and right-hand wings are joined to the centre section (wing stub) to form a complete wing assembly. The four pylons, which will carry the engines, are fitted to the leading edges of the wings at this stage.

At the next stage, the first of the fuselage (or body) sub-assemblies (Section 44) is lowered on to the wing and bolted in position. Also, at this stage, the leading-edge flaps, spoilers (air brakes) and ailerons are fitted to the wings.

A 747 really begins to take on a recognisable form at the next station along the final assembly line, where the forward and aft body sub-assemblies (Sections 41 and 42, and Sections 46 and 48, respectively) are brought in to be joined to the front and rear of the centre body. From hereon the sheer size of everything becomes really apparent, with only the Boeing personnel remaining normal size.

The main structure is completed when the tailplane and elevators (horizontal stabiliser) and the fin and rudder are fitted. The tailplane is of the variable-incidence type (with its angle adjustable for trimming the aircraft's pitch) and it has a span only 15in less than the wing span of the Boeing 247. The 747s are not painted until after assembly and roll-out, being in a protective coat of green primer on the line, but the rudder has to be painted before this because it must be at its final weight when it is balanced before being fitted to the fin. The triple-slotted trailing-edge flaps are now fitted to the wings, followed by the eight big glass-fibre 'canoe' fairings to cover the flap operating mechanism.

Also fitted at this stage is the two-wheel nose landing gear and the unique four-leg main landing gear, so that from now on the aircraft can be moved on its own wheels. The inboard legs of the main landing gear are mounted in the fuselage and the outboard legs are mounted in the wings, and all four legs are fitted with a four-wheel bogie (truck) to spread the weight of the aircraft, enabling it to use runways and taxiways of similar strength to the 707. The inboard bogies are steerable to prevent tyre 'scrubbing' on sharp turns.

Although the aircraft now looks almost complete there is a lot of equipment to install inside and the remaining parts to be fitted to the outside so it is now moved to the first of three 'fitting out' stations on the line. Here, the electrical, hydraulic and cabin air conditioning and pressurisation systems are completed; the flight deck is completed with its flying controls, control panels, instruments and avionics equipment; the passenger cabin is provided with toilets, galleys, wall and ceiling panels, and the 1001 other items to prepare it for human habitation, although the airlines often fit their own carpets and seats after delivery; and the under-floor cargo holds are fitted with handling systems for the cargo and baggage containers. Externally, there are the four main engines to install, each weighing nearly four tons, and the auxiliary power unit (APU), a 1100 h.p. gas turbine, in the rear of the fuselage, which supplies electrical power while the aircraft is on the ground as well as an air supply for cabin air conditioning and for starting the main engines. There are also the finishing touches to be made to the airframe, including the radome covering the weather radar in the nose, the tail cone over the APU, and the landing gear doors. Some big items to be fitted at this stage are the wing-to-body fairings, which are 80ft long and made in sections from glass-fibre honeycomb material, and the wing tips, which are 14ft long, 2ft wide and 16in thick, and are made from aluminium/glass-fibre honeycomb sandwich so that they weigh only 38lb each.

When the aircraft is finally completed, the doors at the end of the assembly-line are opened and the great moment of the roll-out occurs. But the aircraft's first flight is still some way off because once outside there are tests to be made on the systems, including cabin pressurisation. Then the brand new, but bare, 747 is towed over a 60ft wide bridge (spanning a highway) to another part of the site alongside the airport where the paint hangar and pre-flight area are located.

Painting an aircraft the size of a 747 is no small undertaking and a special building was constructed for this purpose, fully equipped with track-mounted spray-gun platforms and overhead heaters to provide controlled drying conditions. The quantity of paint required for one 747 can be quite staggering, especially if the aircraft has a 'white top'. For example, a Pan American 747 requires a total of 76gal – 68 of white, seven of blue for the cheat line and the symbol on the tail, and one of black for the titling (plus a pint of red for the stripes in the US flag on the top of the fin).

Having received its glamour treatment, the aircraft is towed to the flight line where its tanks are filled with fuel; fuelling is through two valves located beneath the leading edge of each wing, between the engines, which allow fuel to be pumped aboard at a rate of 2000gal per minute. Then come the engine tests and further system checks, and finally a visit to the compass-swinging bay where the aircraft is parked on an air-bearing turntable and rotated slowly by a small tractor while the aircraft's compass system is calibrated.

Now the aircraft is ready for its test flights, first by the Boeing test crew and then by the crew who will accept the aircraft on behalf of the airline.

For the ceremonial roll-out of 747 No.1 on September 30, 1968, Boeing cheated a little by painting the aircraft earlier and returning it to the end of the assembly line so that guests did not see a bare aircraft emerging from the main assembly building on that great day but, instead, the world's largest airliner in all its glory, with a white top, red cheat line and fin flash, and blue "Boeing 747" titling, with the appropriate registration N7470. And painted on each side of the nose were the badges of the 27 airlines who had ordered between them 158 of the aircraft. In order of appearance, these airlines were: Pan American (25), Lufthansa (6), Japan Air Lines (6), BOAC (11), TWA (12), Air France (4), Continental Air Lines (3), American Airlines (10), Norwest Orient Airlines (15), United Air Lines (18), Alitalia (4), World Airways (3), Aer Lingus (2), National Airlines (2), KLM (3), Air India (4), Eastern Airlines (4), Delta Air Lines (3), Qantas (4), Swissair (2), Scandinavian Airlines System (2), Braniff

International Airways (2), El Al (2), Air Canada (3), South African Airways (3), Iberia (3) and Sabena (2).

The roll-out of 747 No. 1 was actually a day ahead of schedule, as planned at the start of the programme, but the preparations required for its first flight (including the installation of all the test instrumentation and automatic flight recorder equipment, as well as the usual engine and system checks) took rather longer than anticipated so that the planned first-flight date of December 17, 1968 (the 65th Anniversary of the Wright Brothers' first flight) slipped a little. This was unfortunate from an historical point of view because of the significance of the date but such a happening is not unknown in the aircraft manufacturing world and only Boeing's pride was hurt when the new Queen of the Sky was a little late for her debut.

After the usual high-speed taxi runs along the runway, 747 No. 1 took to the air for the first time from Snohomish/Paine Field on February 9, 1969 in the hands of Jack Waddell, Boeing's senior experimental test pilot, with Brien Wygle, assistant director of flight operations, as co-pilot, and Jess Wallick, as flight engineer. The flight lasted over an hour but was cut short, because of a slight problem with the trailing-edge flaps, and the landing gear was not retracted. However, the second flight was trouble-free and the landing gear was retracted so that the aircraft flew in its proper, 'cleaned-up', state for the first time to show off its sleek lines. After a few more flights to get to know the

The first flight of 747 No. 1, on February 9, 1969, with the aircraft displaying its unique 18-wheel landing gear. (Boeing)

handling characteristics of the huge aircraft, No.1 was flown to Boeing Field, Seattle, the home of Boeing's flight test centre.

Then followed a year of intensive flight testing, with four other 747s joining No.1 at Seattle. No.2, rolled out on February 28, 1969, was the first to be painted in airline colours – the much photographed and appropriately registered N747PA *Clipper America* for Pan American, or rather Pan Am, because the world-famous airline introduced its abbreviated title on this aircraft (to be strictly accurate, N747PA and other Pan Am 747s rolled out during this period had a "Jet Clipper" prefix to their names, like the 707s, but the "Jet" part of the prefix was dropped before the aircraft were delivered). No.4, N731PA for Pan Am, was next to be rolled out on April 23, 1969, but carried "Boeing 747" titles and became the first 747 to be seen abroad when it appeared at the Paris Air Show on June 3, 1969, after flying the 5160 miles from Seattle non-stop in just over 9hr – a few days earlier it had made a 10hr endurance test by flying Seattle – New York – Seattle non-stop to check its specific range. At Paris it was parked alongside Concorde No.1, the first of the Anglo-French supersonic airliners, which gave visitors to the show food for thought as to which way air travel was heading.

The flight-test quintet was completed by No.5, N93101 for TWA, which was rolled out on May 8, 1969, and No.3, N732PA for Pan Am, which was a little late in appearing, on May 16, 1969, because it was fitted with a 32ft long aluminium boom on its nose for gust measurements and was equipped with specialised instrumentation to measure flight loads during excessive manoeuvres as part of the structure verification programme.

Also built during this period were two 747s that would never fly but would play a vital role in the non-flying part of the structure verification programme. This part of the programme consisted of static testing, to determine the strength of the aircraft's structure, and fatigue testing to check the fatigue life of the structure.

For the year-long static test, a structurally complete airframe was located in an extension of the main assembly building at Everett in March 1969 and every part that would be subjected to loads in flight had simulated flight loads applied to it by hydraulic jacks, with the results being measured by strain gauges. Initially, these were proof load tests to satisfy the Federal Aviation Administration (FAA) that the 747 was safe for commercial service, and were a necessary part of the certification programme for the aircraft. After these were successfully completed, the tests were continued from where the proof tests left off to find the ultimate load. The 747 had been designed to have a structural strength at least 50 per cent above proof-test level and therefore loads one and a half times greater than in the proof tests were applied, with similarly successful results. Finally came the test to destruction, which would determine the total strength of the aircraft and indicate the growth potential of the basic design, forming the basis for future increases in the maximum take-off weight to enable more payload to be carried or more fuel for greater range. The mighty bang that ended the static test came in February 1970 when, with its tail sawn off and its wing tips deflected upward 26ft, so that it looked more like a butterfly than a

Boeing, the 747's wing was strained beyond endurance and structural failure occurred – at 116 per cent of the design ultimate load of the aircraft.

The two-year fatigue test was also started in 1969 when another structurally complete airframe was installed in a steel framework on a 3ft thick concrete apron outside the main assembly building adjacent to the static test section. The aim of this programme was to duplicate the stresses experienced in day-to-day airline flying to make certain that no undetected metal fatigue would be encountered in the service life of the aircraft. The programme took the aircraft through the equivalent of 20,000 airline flights (representing 60,000 flying hours or a 20-year life). With sophisticated test equipment, each 'flight' made by the fatigue-test aircraft, comprising taxying, take-off, climb (with cabin pressurisation), cruise, descent (with cabin depressurisation), landing and taxying, could be achieved in about 10min. Instead of being in a water tank, to prevent an explosive failure should any part of the pressurised cabin fail under test, the fuselage was practically filled with plastic granules, with passages left to provide access for inspection of the structure. This lengthy programme continued long after the first 747s entered service in January 1970, with the fatigue-test aircraft accumulating 'flying hours' well ahead of any 747 in service, and was successfully concluded in September 1971. After this, the fatigue-test aircraft was subjected to a programme of fail-safe testing, where primary structure was intentionally cracked or sawn through in 28 critical places, putting the equivalent of 12,000 additional hours in airline flights on the structure to make sure it would continue to operate safely even after being damaged. Changes found necessary from the results of these tests were incorporated in new production aircraft.

Apart from the flight and structure tests, the FAA also required other tests to be conducted on the 747, including proof that the emergency evacuation procedure would enable 500 passengers to escape from the aircraft in the event of an emergency. For this purpose, the 747 has ten double-width doors (five on each side) plus (on early aircraft) a single door on the right-hand side of the upper deck, all equipped with inflatable slides. For the purposes of the evacuation tests, all the windows of the 747 were covered, only emergency (battery) lighting was used in the cabin, and only half the main doors were used. The 'passengers', volunteers of all ages some of whom had never flown, were given the usual pre-flight description of the emergency equipment by a normal cabin staff of 13 stewardesses who, when the order was given to evacuate the aircraft, directed the passengers to the available exits. Several of these tests were made, using different people each time, and the results proved that 500 people could be evacuated from a 747 in 90sec.

The 747 was certificated for commercial passenger service on December 30, 1969. During the 10-month Boeing and FAA flight test programme the five 747s which had taken part had logged more than 1400 flying hours. Four of these aircraft were returned to Everett for refurbishing prior to delivery to their respective airlines (Pan Am or TWA), while 747 No.1 remained in flight-test status with Boeing ready to test new equipment as part of the development programme for the 747.

Into Service

The Spacious Age for modern air travellers began on January 22, 1970 when Pan Am operated its first Boeing 747 commercial service from New York to London. The event had been planned for January 21 but had to be delayed when the specially-chosen 747 No. 10, N735PA *Clipper Young America* developed engine trouble and had to be replaced by No. 11, N736PA *Clipper Victor*, which was quickly re-named *Clipper Young America* for the occasion and operated the inaugural service just a few hours late, departing in the early hours of January 22, hence the conflicting dates appearing in the history books.

Teething troubles are not uncommon during the introductory phase of a new type of airliner, especially one powered by a new type of engine, and the 747, being a particularly interesting new type of airliner, received full coverage from the news media whenever one failed to leave on time or had to return with an engine shut-down. The Pratt & Whitney JT9D engines were troublesome during that first year of 747 operations but the problems were soon diagnosed and modifications introduced. There were also problems with the airframe, especially with some of the new equipment in the passenger cabin, but again modification action reduced the problems in later production aircraft and earlier aircraft were modified to the new standard.

Although these technical problems loomed large at the time, they failed to stop the 747 from having an impressive introductory year. Most new types of airliner are few and far between in their first year of operation while production builds up. Not so the 747. Production had been building up during the second half of 1969 and, although a problem with the installation of the JT9D engines resulted in some aircraft being rolled out without engines, once the supply of modified engines started arriving at Everett the backlog of completed aircraft awaiting engines was soon cleared. And with production reaching its peak rate in March 1970, when one 747 was being rolled out every three working days, the deliveries to airlines reached impressive figures in double-quick time. Within six months of the first commercial service, 55 had been delivered to 11 airlines – besides Pan Am, these were TWA, Lufthansa, Air France, BOAC, Japan Air Lines, Northwest Orient, Alitalia, Continental, American and United. On July 16, 1970, Boeing announced that the 1 millionth passenger had flown on a 747, which set a new record in air transport because it had taken the 707 a year to achieve this magic figure. At this time, an average of 26,000 passengers a day was being carried by 747s, which were serving 32 cities in 12 countries.

By the end of the 747's first year of commercial service, over 100 747s had been delivered to 18 airlines, the additional operators being National, Delta, Iberia, Sabena, Aer Lingus, Braniff and KLM. On that first anniversary,

The 1st class compartment can include Zones A and B, as on this Japan Air Lines' 747, with the staircase to the lounge in the centre. (JAL)

Boeing was able to announce that 747s had carried 6 million passengers, had flown 72 million revenue miles and 15½ billion passenger miles, and that the number of arrivals/departures averaged 2900 a week.

Pan Am took delivery of 25 747s during that first year, introducing them on trans-Atlantic services from New York to Amsterdam, Barcelona, Brussels, Frankfurt, Lisbon, London, Paris and Rome, plus Chicago to London and Frankfurt, Washington and Boston to London, and the polar route from San Francisco and Los Angeles to London and Paris. In addition, the aircraft were introduced on trans-Pacific services from Los Angeles and San Francisco to Honolulu, Tokyo and Hong Kong, and the service from New York to San Juan, Puerto Rico. It was on a Pan Am Flight to San Juan in August 1970 that the first hi-jacking of a 747 occurred, which resulted in N735PA *Clipper Young America* making an un-scheduled stop in Cuba. The following month a more serious hi-jacking of a Pan Am 747 occurred, when Palestinian Arab guerrillas re-routed an Amsterdam-New York flight to Cairo, where the aircraft was blown-up. Fortunately, the passengers and crew were allowed to leave the aircraft first but it meant that N752PA *Clipper Fortune* had a very short life of only four months during which it had logged 1125hr.

The second airline to start 747 services was TWA who got in a 'first' by introducing the aircraft initially on the coast-to-coast route between Los

Angeles and New York in February 1970. The airline's first trans-Atlantic 747 service was operated in March from New York to London. By the end of the first year, TWA had 14 747s, and services had been extended to Paris, Rome and Madrid.

American Airlines also started its 747 operations on the coast-to-coast, New York – Los Angeles route and managed to make an early start, in March 1970, by leasing two aircraft from Pan Am. The first of the airline's own 747s were delivered in mid-1970, and by the end of the first year there were ten in service.

The first foreign airline to start 747 services was Lufthansa, who introduced its aircraft on the Frankfurt – New York route in April 1970. These were joined over the Atlantic in June by Air France 747s on the Paris – New York route and Alitalia 747s on the Rome – New York route.

With the Atlantic taken over by 747s, the Pacific was next. Pan Am also led the way across this ocean by starting its 747 services from Los Angeles to Honolulu in April 1970. Continental followed on the same route in June. Japan Air Lines also started its 747 operations over the Pacific in June, initially on the Tokyo – Honolulu route and extending this shortly afterwards to Los Angeles.

Northwest Orient started 747 operations on its Minneapolis/St Paul – New York route but in July 1970 began a daily service on its New York – Chicago – Seattle – Tokyo route. The following month 747s took over the Minneapolis/St Paul – San Francisco – Honolulu – Tokyo route, which was extended to Taipei, Taiwan, and Hong Kong in September. By the end of the 747's first year of operation the airline had ten 747s in service.

The final airline to introduce 747s over the Pacific in the summer of 1970 was United, who made a start on the San Francisco – Honolulu route and later extended services to US domestic routes, including coast-to-coast. United had nine 747s in service by the end of the first year.

Two other US domestic operators started 747 operations in October 1970; National on its Miami – New York and Miami – Los Angeles routes, and Delta on its Atlanta – Dallas – Los Angeles route.

To round off the 747's introductory year, Iberia started services on its Madrid – New York route in December 1970, Eastern leased three of Pan Am's 747s during that winter and introduced them on its New York – San Juan, and New York and Chicago – Miami, routes in January 1971, and Braniff started a daily shuttle on its Dallas/Fort Worth – Honolulu route on January 15, 1971 with 747 No. 100 (the colourful N601BN, later to become famous as the original Big Orange but advertised at that time as "747 Braniff Place, the Most Exclusive Address in the Sky").

Although Aer Lingus, BOAC, KLM and Sabena took delivery of some of their 747s during the year they did not start operating them until after the 747's first year was over.

For all its early faults, the 747 had lost no time in becoming established on the major long-haul air routes of the world and, in the process, had made a giant leap for air transport.

Not everyone was pleased at its coming, of course, especially the managements of some of the major airports, where extension of terminal buildings to accommodate the larger groups of passengers was not done at Boeing speed so that some of the buildings were not ready in time for the first arrivals. The critics, too, had their say, but many had assumed that a 500-seater was being introduced whereas the 747s which entered service in 1970 had seating for only 350 or so passengers, and not every seat on every flight was filled. The 747s were also less noisy than expected, making less noise than turbo-fan-powered 707s even though their engines produced twice the power (and the big-fan engines made virtually no smoke).

The sheer size of the 747 is most noticeable when the aircraft is viewed close-up from ground level, and this was the view that most passengers got during that introductory year because air bridges (covered-in extensible walkways) between the terminal buildings and the aircraft were not available at many airports so passengers boarded the 747s up mobile steps from ground level. The climb up 25 or so steps to the 16-ft main-deck level of a 747 (compared with about 15 steps up to a 707's cabin) might be considered sufficiently breath-taking but the view that greeted passengers through the double-width entrance door was equally so. Here was a cabin that was totally different from those of earlier jet airliners, gone was the 'tube look'; this was high, wide and handsome, with a flat ceiling over 8ft high spanning the 20ft width between near-vertical walls. If the 186ft long cabin of the 747 had been arranged in the 'open-plan' style of earlier jet airliners, with doors, toilets and galleys at each end, the sight greeting boarding passengers might have been rather off-putting, like viewing an empty theatre from the stage or, if they were the last to board, seeing nothing but an ocean of faces. But the 747 was different. A clear area was required at each of the ten doors, for emergency-evacuation reasons, and these conveniently divided the cabin into five zones, lettered A to E from the nose. The break-down of the interior into separate compartments was completed by locating galleys and groups of toilets in the centre of the cabin at each door break.

A unique feature of the 747 is that, because the flight deck is located on a level above the main deck, the passenger cabin extends right into the nose of the aircraft. This is the quietest part of the cabin and was therefore selected for the first-class compartment. Up to 24 passengers can be seated in this Zone A, which has double seats along each side at 40in pitch, and the spiral staircase to the upper-deck lounge is located in the centre of the cabin at the rear of the zone. A galley for serving the first-class meals is located immediately behind the spiral staircase so that cabin dividers can be fitted at this point to make Zone A a separate first-class compartment, or the compartment can be extended to include Zone B with the cabin dividers at the second door break. The Pan Am and TWA 747s, for example, had a further 34 first-class passengers in Zone B, making a total of 58.

Economy-class passengers in Zones C, D and E had seating arrangements during that introductory year which were far more spacious than they had ever had on the earlier jet airliners. With nine-abreast seating: arranged three, four, two, with two aisles, there was space to accommodate seats which were 2in wider and had wider armrests than those used previously. And the two wide

Meals and movies help to relieve the boredom of long over-ocean flights, and the screens on 747s are bigger than those of earlier aircraft. (TWA)

aisles, with cross-over aisles at each door break, provided passengers with space for strolling to stretch their legs and an easier access to the toilets. There never seem to be enough toilets on an aircraft, especially at 'wakey-wakey' time after an overnight trans-Atlantic flight, but at least on the 747s they were more numerous, the total depending on the airline but generally between 12 and 14, so that queues for them were not so long.

The three economy-class zones on TWA 747s had seating for 284 passengers, with 92 in Zone C, 78 in Zone D and 114 in Zone E. To simplify seat-finding during boarding all the zones were colour-coded – gold for first class (Zones A and B) and blue, red and green for Zones C, D and E, respectively and passengers were given a boarding pass which was of the appropriate zone colour as well as bearing the seat row number and actual seat number; economy-class boarding passes also bore a prefix letter, from C to H, which indicated the aisle in which the seat was located. In this way, passengers could be boarded through the front doors in groups according to the colour of their boarding passes, so that, for example, passengers at the rear of the aircraft could be boarded first by calling those with green boarding passes, and time allowed for them to walk through the other zones before calling passengers in those zones. Pan Am 747s had accommodation for 299 economy-class passengers, and a similar colour-code system was used for boarding them.

Serving meals to so many passengers could have been a major problem but, by locating six or so galleys at strategic points throughout the cabin and having two aisles for the trolleys (or carts as some airlines call them) the cabin service was generally better. In fact, with the reduced distance between galley and passenger, TWA dropped the 'meals on wheels' service and went for a personalised service, enabling passengers to eat when they were ready to do so within normal meal periods. Pan Am also withdrew its carts after a few months, changing to stewardess-carried trays. The number of cabin staff varied between airlines and routes but was usually around 15, who performed their duties under the watchful eye of a cabin services manager or someone with similar rank but different title, like Air France's chef de cabine.

The zoned passenger cabin of the 747 could have been designed especially for in-flight entertainment, with the rear walls of the dividing galleys and toilet groups serving as ideal locations for film screens, which are twice the size of those in earlier aircraft. Each zone is equipped with its own screen and in TWA 747s (and later those of some other airlines) a choice of film (or movie) was available, one for general audiences (suitable for children) being shown in some zones and a 'mature movie' in other zones. The soundtrack is heard through headphones so that passengers not wishing to watch the film can doze undisturbed; the headphones can also be used to receive a variety of music and audio entertainment programmes when a film show is not in progress, a selector switch (with a reading light switch and a cabin service call-button) being located in the armrest of each seat. Although film shows are not appreciated by all passengers, when they are interspersed with meals they can help to relieve the boredom of over-ocean flying for the majority of passengers, especially when flight times of 8 to 10hr are involved. Zoning of the passenger cabin also simplifies the separation of non-smokers from smokers, and most airlines introduced separate zones for these with seats being selected to suit at check-in time.

Another unique feature of the 747 is its upper-deck compartment behind the flight deck which, during the 747's introductory year, was used by almost all airlines as a lounge for first-class passengers. Up to 16 passengers could be accommodated up there during flight and, being equipped with a bar, it proved as popular as the downstairs lounge in the earlier Stratocruiser. Some interior designers were allowed to apply their talents to the full in this compartment, devising a decor to suit either the nationality of the airline, like Japan Air Lines' Teahouse of the Sky, or a particular atmosphere, such as Braniff's International Lounge, which the airline described as being 'like an intimate club overlooking the world'.

Baggage was another subject given much thought in the design of the 747. Overhead lockers (or stowage bins) fitted throughout the main cabin accommodate a lot of the carry-on baggage of the passengers, thereby reducing the usual congestion around their feet, especially in the economy-class zones. A container system was designed for the main baggage, the containers being packed with baggage in the terminal building and simply loaded into the front underfloor hold when taken out to the aircraft, avoiding the handling of individual cases at that stage which could have been very time-consuming with such quantities. The large doors to the underfloor holds are opened and closed electrically, and the holds are equipped with a container handling system to simplify loading and unloading.

In addition to 350 passengers and their baggage, a 747 could also carry 20 tons of cargo and mail, more than half the total payload of a 707 freighter. This cargo is packed into 14 containers and loaded into the rear underfloor hold or, if it is too big to fit into a container it can be loaded into a smaller bulk compartment at the rear of the aircraft. The containers in the two main holds are interchangeable so that, if there is not a full complement of passengers, some of the 16 baggage containers in the front hold can also be filled with cargo. With the handling equipment aboard the aircraft, and power loaders, transports and tugs on the ground, all 30 containers can be loaded or unloaded in less than 15min.

The flight deck on the 747 is surprisingly small for such a large aircraft but it was designed for a crew of three (captain, first officer and flight engineer), the navigator carried aboard all earlier long-range jet airliners having been displaced by the inertial navigation system (INS). Adapted from a system developed for the Apollo moon flights and nuclear submarines, the INS is completely independent of ground aids and is highly accurate. By means of push-buttons, the pilot can insert into the equipment the latitude and longitude of the flight's terminal points and up to eight waypoints (for en route course changes). The INS is linked to the autopilot, and in flight the pilot monitors a display showing present position, ground speed, heading, distance and time to

The flight deck on a 747 accommodates a flight crew of three – captain, first officer and flight engineer. (Boeing)

next waypoint or destination, and other navigational data. Two INS sets are fitted as standard and a third set can be fitted as a stand-by which can take-over should one or both of the primary sets ever fail.

Another unusual item of equipment which could be fitted to 747s as an option was the SATCOM aerial, located in a 'bump' at the rear of the 'hump' on the top of the fuselage, which could be used to relay radio messages via communication satellites. Otherwise the 747s were equipped with all the latest avionics and instrumentation as befits a modern airliner, and its automatic flight control system provided for automatic landings to Category II as a basic and Category IIIA as an option.

The primary flying controls consist of an inboard and outboard aileron on each side, a two-section elevator on each side, a two-section rudder and a variable-incidence tailplane, and are power actuated from four hydraulic systems so arranged that each of the three attitude axes (roll, pitch and yaw) is powered by all four systems. These systems also provide hydraulic pressure for landing gear and wing flap actuation, spoiler deployment, wheel-brake operation, and nose gear and body gear steering. The electrical system has a similar reserve of power, with four generators driven by the main engines in flight or two generators on the auxiliary power unit (APU) providing power when the aircraft is on the ground.

747 Varieties

Over four hundred Boeing 747s were produced during the ten years which followed the entry into airline service of the first aircraft in January 1970. Although at first glance most of the 747s rolled out at the end of 1979 appeared to be the same as the early aircraft, a closer inspection would reveal the many changes that had been introduced during the years as a result of a continuing development programme. Apart from the major changes to provide variants for specific duties, such as the Freighter, Convertible (passenger or freighter), Short Range, Combi (combination passenger and freighter) and Special Performance (very long range), there had been numerous other changes to the basic design, such as the introduction of Pratt & Whitney engines of increased power and engines from other manufacturers (General Electric and Rolls-Royce), increases in the maximum take-off weight and fuel capacity, and changes to the passenger accommodation to suit the ever-changing requirements of the airlines.

When the airlines first started ordering 747s in the mid-1960s, the only model available was the basic version so no model numbers were allocated. Most of these airlines were already operating other types of Boeing jet airliners (707s or 727s) and the customer identification number which had been used for these, to indicate changes from the basic configuration to meet their individual requirements, was carried over to the 747 orders, so that Pan Am aircraft were referred to as the 747-21, TWA aircraft as the 747-31, BOAC aircraft as the 747-36, etc. Any new Boeing customers were identified in a similar manner; to avoid lengthy numbers, this original series ended at 99 and later customers (for the 707, 727, 737 or 747) were identified in the 'alpha-numeric' series A1 to A9, B1 to B9, etc.

Some Convertible (C) and Freighter (F) versions of the basic 747 were ordered in the mid-1960s and these were identified by a suffix after the customer's number, so that a 747C for World Airways was a 747-73C and a 747F for Pan Am was a 747-21F. These orders were later either cancelled or changed to passenger versions because the empty weight of the basic version had increased above that planned and this reduced the aircraft's weight-lifting ability in the freight-carrying role while the maximum take-off weight was restricted to 710,000lb.

In June 1968, before the first 747 had been completed, Boeing announced the availability of the 747B, a developed version with an increased maximum take-off weight of 775,000lb with improved payload/range performance. This improvement made the Freighter a viable proposition again so the C and F versions were offered at this increased weight.

The first 747-200B – No. 88, N611US for Northwest Orient – took to the air for the first time on October 11, 1970.   (Boeing)

Before the first 747 deliveries were made in December 1969, Boeing introduced the current 'hundred series' model numbering system to identify the different take-off weights and any future major changes, in a similar fashion to the system used on the other Boeing jet airliners. The basic version of the 747 then became the 747-100, with a Pan Am aircraft being identified as the 747-121, etc., and the 747B became the 747-200B (or 747-200C or 747-200F), with a Northwest Orient aircraft being identified as the 747-251B, etc.

Individual aircraft are identified by a constructor's number which remains with the aircraft throughout its life, regardless of changes in ownership or country of registration (and, therefore, changes of its registration markings). When 707s, 727s, 737s and 747s are ordered from Boeing each aircraft is allocated a five-figure constructor's number from a common series. These numbers then provide the means of identifying individual 747s before and after construction but unfortunately they do not follow in strict numerical order, because of the 707s, 727s and 737s in between, and of those that are used the aircraft are not necessarily constructed in ascending order and are subject to cancellation before construction. Throughout this book, therefore, a line number is used to identify individual 747s, because these numbers are allocated to an aircraft only when its major components are brought together for final assembly, and they have been issued to 747s in strict numerical order from No. 1 onwards. A production list at the end of this book serves as a cross-reference between line numbers and constructor's numbers.

There was no prototype 747, so 747 No. 1 was the first production 747-100 and, although it has remained as a Boeing-owned development and demonstration aircraft, it has always been referred to as a 747-121, the same as 747 Nos. 2, 3 and 4 which were the first aircraft for Pan Am. As mentioned earlier, 747 No. 1 was rolled out on September 30, 1968, followed by No. 2 in February 1969 and Nos. 3, 4 and 5 in April and May 1969 – No. 5 being the first 747-131 for TWA. These five aircraft were used in the flight test programme which continued throughout 1969 and resulted in the 747 obtaining its Certificate of Airworthiness on December 30, 1969.

By the end of **1969**, 747 No. 36 – the first 747-143 for Alitalia – had been rolled out, and the production rate had reached five a month. 747 Nos. 6 to 35 were all 747-100s and destined to be the start of the big fleets of Pan Am, TWA, Lufthansa, Air France, BOAC, Northwest Orient and Japan Air Lines (JAL). Because of an installation problem with the Pratt & Whitney JT9D-3 engines, some of these aircraft were rolled out without engines and spent some time parked on the flight line at Everett awaiting modified engines. However, the worst of the problems had been overcome by the end of the year, and 747 Nos. 6 and 7 (N733PA and N734PA) were delivered to Pan Am, and 747 No. 8 (N93102) to TWA, during December 1969 for crew training in preparation for the start of commercial services the following month.

Deliveries of the 747 began in earnest in January 1970 and Pan Am had five of its aircraft when scheduled services began on January 22.

Production of the 747 reached the peak rate of seven a month in March 1970 and continued at that rate until the end of the year to satisfy the initial demand for the aircraft. Nos. 37 to 74 were rolled out between **January and June 1970**, all being 747-100s and mainly additions to the growing fleets of Pan Am, TWA, Lufthansa, Air France, BOAC, Northwest and JAL, but also including the first aircraft for Continental, American, United, National and Delta.

A fifth engine was fitted to 747 No. 1 at the beginning of 1970 so that a test and certification programme could be conducted on the carriage of a complete spare engine (less its big fan) beneath the left-hand wing between No. 2 engine and the fuselage. This simplified the ferrying of engines of this size which would otherwise have to be dismantled into sub-assemblies so that they could fit into the underfloor cargo hold. The installation was certificated in March 1970 and made available to airlines as an option.

The first 747-200B, 747 No. 88 (N611US for Northwest Orient), was among the 42 747s rolled out during the period **July to December 1970**. A further four of this new model were also included, the first aircraft for KLM (No. 96 – PH-BUA), Swissair (No. 112 – HB-IGA), Scandinavian Airlines System (SAS) (No. 114 – SE-DDL, appropriately named *Huge Viking*) and JAL (No. 116 – JA8104). All other aircraft rolled out during this six-month period of peak production, Nos. 75 to 116, with the aforementioned exceptions, were additional 747-100s for Pan Am, TWA, Air France, BOAC, Northwest, American, United, National and Delta, plus the first 747-100s for Iberia, Aer Lingus, Sabena and Air Canada. Also rolled out during this period was 747 No.100, which was the orange-painted N601BN for Braniff, later to become the 747 with the highest time (or the most utilised).

As mentioned earlier, the **747-200B** had an increased maximum take-off weight of 775,000lb, allowing an increased payload or an increased fuel capacity of US51,430gal. The initial production aircraft was powered by JT9D-3AW engines, the fully-modified JT9D-3 (the JT9D-3A then becoming available for 747-100s) with water injection to increase take-off thrust to 45,000lb, but later aircraft were powered by the JT9D-7 which produced 45,500lb thrust dry. The external dimensions and appearance of the 747-200B remained the same as the 747-100 but the structure and landing gear were strengthened to allow operation at the increased weight. During tests, 747 No.88 set a world record in November 1970 when it took off at a gross weight of 820,700lb, exceeding by some 10 tons a record established earlier in the year by a US Air Force C-5A Galaxy.

Pan Am's 747-100s were returned one by one to Boeing from November 1970 for a refurbishing programme 'to clean up the nitty-gritty technical problems that developed in the first year's operations'. Major work included fitting the aircraft with JT9D-3AW engines and increasing the maximum take-off weight to 735,000lb, adding another 460 miles to the aircraft's normal range of 4,500 miles or increasing the payload by 15 per cent. Other work included modifications to the landing gear, flaps, fuel system, doors and passenger cabin entertainment system. When they emerged, the aircraft were designated (by Pan Am, not Boeing) the 747-100A. These modifications were also embodied on some other early 747-100s but without the change of designation.

Between **January and June 1971** the production rate was reduced slightly from seven to five a month, indicating that the initial demand had been met and also that there had been a slowing down in the upward trend of the world's air traffic graph because of world economic conditions resulting in less orders. Of the 34 747s rolled out during this period (Nos.117 to 150) three 747-100s were found to be surplus to their airline's requirements; No.123 (N602BN for Braniff) and Nos.131 and 142 (N658PA and N659PA, respectively, for Pan Am), and were placed in storage at Boeing's Wichita factory. The 747-200B began to take a higher percentage of places on the assembly lines, this batch including two each for existing operators Northwest, KLM and JAL; two each for new operators Alitalia (its first 747-200B), Air India and Qantas; a second aircraft for Swissair; and the first aircraft for Condor, Lufthansa (its first 747-200B), and El Al. The 747-100s rolled out during this period were additional aircraft for Pan Am, American, Air Canada, United, Continental and BOAC.

The first change to the external appearance of the 747 occurred at this time when No.147, the first 747-200B for Qantas (VH-EBA), was rolled out with an extended upper-deck compartment equipped with ten windows on each side instead of the usual three. The external dimensions of the 'hump' remained the same but an internal re-arrangement extended the length of this compartment by 6ft to 25ft and increased the accommodation for take-off and landing from 8 to 16 passengers, and in flight from 16 to as many as 25 passengers. On Qantas aircraft the compartment was fitted out as a Captain Cook Lounge (with appropriate nautical decor) for first-class passengers, but the modification was the first stage towards changing this compartment from an in-flight lounge for first-class passengers to one having saleable seats and, in some cases, a change of class from first to economy. Some later aircraft continued to have the smaller compartment, to match earlier aircraft in an airline's fleet, but most aircraft had the internal extension even if they did not have the additional windows fitted (or, if provision was made for the windows, they were blanked). This accounts for the variations in the external appearance of aircraft built at this time. Some earlier aircraft were later returned to Boeing for modification and therefore also have the extended compartment with the additional windows. Another interesting feature on the Qantas 747-200Bs was the location of the economy-class galley on the 'lower deck', occupying part of the rear underfloor cargo hold, with cart and personnel lifts (or elevators) linking it with a service centre on the main deck. As Qantas said at the time, this leaves more space for passengers on the main deck and protects them from cooking smells and 'kitchen clatter'. This galley location is an optional feature and has not been adopted by many airlines because of the loss of cargo space.

El Al's first 747-200B, No.140 (4X-AXA), was built before the upper-deck modification was introduced on the assembly lines, so had the original upper-deck compartment, but the airline introduced a change in the normal order of things by equipping the compartment as a first-class cabin for eight passengers and devoting the whole of the main deck to economy class (seating 393 passengers). This aircraft was later returned to Boeing to have the extension and additional windows.

Condor Flugdienst, the charter subsidiary of Lufthansa, also introduced a different interior arrangement in its first 747-200B, No.128 (D-ABYF, later to become better known as *Fritz* to its friends). Being the first 747 for a charter operator, it had an all-economy configuration for 470 passengers, with ten-abreast seating on the main deck and eight passengers in the upper-deck compartment. Like El Al's first aircraft, *Fritz* was built before the upper-deck modification and was later returned to Boeing for the modification, which increased the accommodation upstairs to 16 passengers.

Technical developments at this time included certification of the 747 in February 1971 for Category IIIA automatic landings, zero decision height and 700ft runway visibility, made possible by fitting a triple-channel, fail-operational auto-pilot system.

Production of the 747 was reduced from five to three a month between **July and December 1971**. Of the 28 aircraft rolled out during this period (Nos.151 to 178), 16 were 747-200Bs – additional aircraft for KLM, Qantas, Northwest, El Al, JAL and SAS, and the first aircraft for South African Airways, Iberia (its first 747-200B) and Transportes Aereos Portugueses (TAP). Of the other 12 aircraft, 11 were 747-100s, all additional aircraft for TWA, Delta, JAL, BOAC, Air France and United.

The outstanding aircraft built during this period was the first **747-200F** **(Freighter)**, No.168 (D-ABYE for Lufthansa), which was rolled out in October 1971. Although basically a 747-200B, this variant was easily recognisable from the outside because it had no windows and only two of the usual ten doors, located front and rear on the left-hand side. However, the major feature of this variant was the nose door, the whole of the nose in front of the flight deck opening upward under electrical power to allow straight-in loading and unloading of cargo in all shapes and sizes. The interior of the main-deck compartment is a bare shell surrounding an unobstructed nose-to-tail hold with over 17,000 cubic feet of 8ft high cargo volume, three time the volume of a 707 freighter. The main-deck floor is strengthened to take heavier localised loads and is equipped with a mechanised cargo-handling system, consisting of electrically-powered rollers located along the centre lines of each of two parallel tracks which extend almost the full length of the compartment. The 747 was designed from the outset with the ability to accommodate 8ft high by 8ft wide containers in two rows down the main length of the compartment and these containers can have lengths in multiples of 10ft up to a maximum of 40ft. Up to six 40ft long containers (plus a few smaller ones) can be carried in one load.

Normal loads for air freighters are small containers and cargo loaded on pallets, but the nose-loading 747-200F can also accommodate loads of unusual size and length. Drilling pipes and casing or other ducting in lengths up to 180ft and diameters up to 8ft can be carried, and as many as 73 Volkswagens have been loaded aboard the Lufthansa aircraft, including 14 in the front and rear underfloor cargo holds which are also available for containerised or palletised cargo.

Two men, a loadmaster at the nose and a loader in the interior of the aircraft, can complete the loading or unloading of a 747 Freighter in 30min. The loadmaster has a control panel to operate the various sections of the cargo-handling system. Because the fuselage tapers at the nose, only a single track is fitted in the entrance and the containers or pallets are directed from here on to either the left-hand or right-hand track by steerable powered-roller units. Using local control panels provided along each side of the compartment, the loader controls the movement of the container or pallet to its stowed position. A scissor-lift platform is used to raise the containers or pallets from ground level to main-deck height.

The 747-200F could carry a maximum payload of 260,000lb nearly 2,900 miles, or a reduced payload of 200,000lb nearly 4,000 miles, which is well beyond trans-Atlantic range. The normal flight crew is three but the upper-deck compartment can be used to accommodate additional crew members, for relief purposes, and is equipped with a toilet and small galley. Because there is no spiral staircase fitted in this variant to provide access from the main deck, a retractable ladder is installed for this purpose. The usual crew door is also fitted on the right-hand side of the upper deck behind the flight deck.

Maximum take-off weight of the first 747-200F was 775,000lb and power was provided by Pratt & Whitney JT9D-7W engines with a take-off rating of 45,500lb thrust dry or 47,900lb thrust wet (i.e. with water injection).

The first 747-200F – No. 168, D-ABYE for Lufthansa – differed from passenger aircraft in having a nose door and no windows.
(Lufthansa)

The more powerful JT9D-7 engines had been fitted first to 747-200B No.154 (ZS-SAL for South African Airways) which had then been used for the certification tests. Another engine development occurring at this time was the testing of fixed-lip engine air intakes (eliminating the blow-in doors around earlier intakes) to reduce engine noise at take-off.

It was during the years 1971 to 1973 that the real Spacious Age for modern air travellers occurred. The 747 had been designed to be oversize at the start of commercial services and to be the correct size for the market after a few years of service, but this planning was based on a steady growth in air traffic. Unfortunately, there was a slow-down in the rate of growth during these years because of the world economic situation and this resulted in 'over-capacity' becoming the 'in' phrase of the time. However, the air travellers benefitted from this because many airlines removed some of the surplus seats and equipped the 747 main decks with small lounges in both first- and economy-class (or coach) zones, and offered these in their advertising as an inducement to would-be customers. As an example, in the 747 Luxury Liners of American Airlines a lounge, complete with stand-up bar, occupied the full cabin width at the rear of Zone E, and the finishing touch was added later with the introduction of a piano, which proved to be very popular; in the first-class a 'table for four' could be booked for dinner or card playing, etc. Pan Am also introduced its well-

48

known dining-room service on the main deck before transferring it to the upper-deck compartment.

Continental's 747 Proud Birds of the Pacific (a rare species, which became extinct in December 1973) had the lowest seating capacity of them all with a total of 290 passengers (reduced from 339). These were arranged in an unusual (for the time) three-class configuration – first-, coach- and economy- classes. The 57 first-class passengers were in Zones A and B, and had the use in flight of an upstairs Diamond Head Lounge; the 145 coach passengers were in Zones C and D, both equipped with four-seat mini-lounges; and the 88 economy passengers were in Zone E, at the rear of which was an eight-seat Ponape Lounge for both coach and economy passengers. Coach passengers had a normal meal service, whereas economy passengers, who paid $10 less for their flights between Los Angeles and Honolulu, could purchase a sandwich meal and small bottle of wine for $1.50.

During the period **January to June 1972** production of the 747 was reduced to two a month, a rate which was to remain until April 1978. The 16 aircraft rolled out during this period (Nos.179 to 194) comprised 11 747-200Bs additional aircraft for Lufthansa, JAL, Air India, Condor, TAP and Alitalia, and 5 747-100s – additional aircraft for BOAC, JAL and United.

The **200th 747** (N28903/F-BPVI for Air France) was rolled out in September 1972 but, because some earlier aircraft had been retained for tests or remained undelivered, the aircraft that took part in the ceremony in April 1973 for handing over the 200th 747 actually delivered was 747 No.212 (4X-AXC for El Al).

In addition to No.200, 10 other 747s were rolled out between **July and December 1972** (Nos.195 to 199 and Nos.201 to 205). These were additional 747-100s for JAL, Air France and United, and additional 747-200Bs for Qantas, JAL and South African Airways, plus two for the US Air Force (Nos.202 and 204).

Apart from their military markings, the US Air Force-aircraft appeared from the outside to be ordinary 747-200Bs, but under the designation **E4A** (E for electronic warfare) they were later flown to Greenville, Texas, to be fitted out by E-Systems Inc. with a special interior and communications equipment to suit them for duty as advanced airborne command posts. These first two aircrafts were powered by Pratt & Whitney JT9D-7W engines.

During the period **January to June 1973**, 13 747s were rolled out (Nos.206 to 218). These were additional 747-100s for United, BOAC and Air Canada, additional 747-200Bs for El Al and Qantas, and the first 747-200Bs for Korean Air Lines, Olympic Airways of Greece and Singapore Airlines, plus the first two 747-200Cs for World Airways (Nos. 209 and 211, appropriately registered N747WA and N748WA, respectively).

At first glance, the **747-200C** (Convertible) looks like a passenger-carrying 747-200B, because it has windows along the main and upper decks, but it also has the nose door and strengthened floor of the 747-200F and the interior can be converted to suit either passenger-carrying or freighter roles. Because of the nose door, the Convertible differs externally from the 747-200B in having only

The first 747-200C (Convertible) – No. 209, N747WA for World Airways – had the Freighter's nose door but also windows for when carrying passengers.
(Boeing)

86 windows along each side of the main deck (including one in each door) instead of 88 – two windows are missing from each side of the nose where the nose door joins the main fuselage.

The conversion of a 747-200C from one role to another is no easy task and should not be confused with the type of conversion possible with specially-equipped quick-change (QC) versions of the Boeing 727 and 737 which can be converted in an hour so that they can carry passengers during the day and cargo at night for maximum utilisation. The time required to convert a 747-200C is measured in days rather than hours but it is still an economical proposition if it means that an airline can perform both types of operation with one aircraft instead of needing two aircraft, one for each role. In the case of World Airways, the aircraft were used initially for trans-Atlantic passenger charter flights during the summer of 1973 and were then transferred to military cargo charters for the US Air Force during the following winter. A similar case occurred later with El Al 747-200Cs, because this airline has a peak in passenger traffic during summer months and a peak in cargo traffic in winter months when it is called on to assist in the export of Israeli agricultural products.

Conversion from an all-passenger to an all-cargo configuration involves first the removal of the passenger kit, which consists of the seats, carpets, spiral staircase, toilets, galleys, partitions, overhead stowage bins, life rafts and passenger escape slides. Then comes the installation of the cargo handling kit, which comprises the twin tracks of rollers, drive units, guides and loading controls, plus the retractable ladder to the upper deck, as fitted in the 747-200F. The Boeing estimate for the minimum time required to complete the conversion was 24hr, using a crew of 35 men working in shifts. This was put to the test, in a typical 'rush job' for a charter company, when in mid-May 1974 (at the start of the passenger-carrying season) there was an immediate need in Japan for 100 large pieces of oil-drilling equipment which were in Pittsburg, USA. World Airways was awarded the job and a 747-200C was positioned to the company's maintenance base at Oakland, California, on May 12, where 35 men working in shifts against the clock managed to complete the conversion in 20hr. The aircraft was then flown to Pittsburg to pick up the load, which included two 46ft long pipe assemblies each weighing 33,000lb, a crown assembly which was 20ft long by just under 10ft wide and weighed 28,000lb, and eight pieces each 40ft long. No special loading equipment was available so each item of cargo was first placed on a flat-bed truck which was then hoisted by two cranes to the 16ft sill height of the aircraft's main deck. The longer items were strapped to several pallets, to simplify the task of handling them once aboard the aircraft, and required the use of a third crane at the remote end when loading; the crown assembly cleared the nose-door opening by less than 2½in. The total payload for the flight was 160,000lb.

During the 8½hr non-stop return flight from Tokyo to Oakland, the cargo crew who had flown with the load to supervise unloading in Japan, began the reverse conversion back to the all-passenger configuration by dismantling the cargo-handling equipment and removing the power drive units. In this way, when the reverse conversion was completed at Oakland it took the 35 men (working shifts) only 27hr, instead of the minimum time estimated by Boeing of 36hr, and the aircraft was back in passenger service on May 18.

In the all-passenger configuration, the 747-200Cs of World Airways accommodated 461 passengers in an all-economy arrangement with ten-abreast seating on the main deck and 16 seats in the upper deck compartment. On one charter flight from Toronto to Rome, the aircraft was full and there were also 32 infants in arms, making a total of 493. The 747-200C can also be operated in a mixed traffic configuration, in which arrangement the cargo would be in the forward zones and a cabin divider would hide this from the view of the passengers in the rear zones.

These first 747-200Cs had a maximum take-off weight of 775,000lb and were powered by Pratt & Whitney JT9D-7AW engines which were rated at 46,950lb thrust, dry, or 48,750lb thrust with water injection.

The JT9D-7A engines had been certificated for use after being tested on 747 No.212 (4X-AXC for El Al) which, as mentioned earlier, became the 200th 747 to be delivered, in April 1973. The extra power of the JT9D-7A engines enabled the maximum take-off weight of the 747-200B to be increased for the first time from 775,000 to 785,000lb.

Another engine 'event' which took place during the first half of 1973 was the first flight on June 26 of 747 No.1 re-engined with General Electric CF6-50D engines of 51,000lb thrust. At the time Boeing introduced the model number 747-300 to distinguish this variant from Pratt & Whitney powered aircraft but this was subsequently dropped and the choice of engine treated as an option.

During the period **July to December 1973**, 11 747s were rolled out (Nos.219 to 229), being additional 747-100s for British Airways (the new name for BOAC) and Air France, additional 747-200Bs for Singapore and Olympic and first 747-200Bs for CP Air of Canada, plus the first two 747-100SRs for JAL, Nos.221 (JA8117) and 229 (JA8118).

The **747-100SR (Short Range)** is intended to fill the requirement for a high-capacity airliner on routes as short as 200 miles. It is basically a 747-100 in which the structure and landing gear have been strengthened to permit it to make 52,000 landings in 20 years; this means that it can average six to seven take-off/landing cycles per day compared with three per day for the standard long-range 747s. However, the normal 747-100 fuel capacity of US47,210gal is provided so that these aircraft can be used on long-range operations if required. The maximum take-off weight of this variant can therefore vary from 520,000lb for short-range flights to 735,000lb for long-range flights.

Although capable of carrying up to 537 passengers in a high-density seating arrangement, when the 747-100SRs entered service with Japan Air Lines they carried a maximum of 498 passengers (an all-time high for the period), being 482 economy class seated ten abreast on the main deck and 16 economy class in the upper deck compartment (the latter seats, having more space, are assigned by the airline to preferred customers, VIPs and frequent travellers). The aircraft were introduced on JAL's busy domestic routes from Tokyo to Osaka (approximately 250 miles), Sapporo (510 miles) and Fukuoka (550 miles), Osaka to Fukuoka (300 miles), and a regional service from Tokyo to Okinawa (965 miles). The busiest route was Tokyo to Sapporo, which had up to ten return SR flights a day in summer. One of the interesting features of these flights is that most passengers are on one-day business trips so have no baggage, which leaves most of the underfloor holds available for cargo.

Externally there is no way of distinguishing a 747-100SR from a 747-100. The JAL aircraft are powered by JT9D-7AW engines, the same as those that power the airline's later standard 747s, but on short-range operations these engines can be operated at the reduced power of 43,500lb thrust for longer life.

The complete range of 747 models and variants available at the time was included among the 13 747s rolled between **January and June 1974** (Nos.230 to 242). One was a 747-100 (an additional aircraft for Air Canada), six were 747-200Bs (additional aircraft for Qantas, JAL, TAP and Singapore), three were additional 747-100SRs for JAL, one was the third 747-200C for World Airways, one was the third E4A for the US Air Force, and the final one (No.242) was the first 747-200F for Seaboard World Airlines.

A change of engines was the notable feature of the third E4A (No.232). This one was powered by General Electric CF6-50E engines (or the F103-GE-100, as the US Air Force call them) which have a take-off thrust of 52,500lb. These engines were then specified for all E4A (and the later E4B) aircraft, and the two earlier aircraft which had been powered by Pratt & Whitney JT9D-7W engines were later returned to the factory to have the General Electric engines fitted.

The winter of 1973/74 was the time of the first OPEC-inspired oil price crisis, with its associated period of inflation and economic gloom. This resulted in cut-backs to air services generally, the withdrawal of some 747s from service (to be placed into storage or put up for sale), and getting the maximum use out of the remaining aircraft. It was at this time that the extra space of the Spacious Age began to disappear, with the gradual withdrawal of lounges from the main decks of 747s, first from the economy/coach zones and then from first class, to allow more seats to be installed.

One idea that had been considered earlier and now came into its own was to convert existing passenger-carrying 747s into combined passenger/cargo carriers by fitting a large cargo door on the left-hand side of the main deck just behind the wing. This became known as the **Side Cargo Door (SCD)** and its introduction on new production aircraft led to a new variant, the 747-200B Combi (combined passenger and cargo), which was to become popular in later years. The first existing aircraft to have the SCD modification were the two 747-100s of Sabena, which were returned to the factory at the beginning of 1974.

The SCD enabled six pallets of cargo, or containers of similar size, to be carried in the rear of the main cabin (Zone E) and reduced the passenger accommodation from a total of 365 (32 first class and 333 economy class) to 242 (28 first class and 214 economy class, but with first class passengers still having the use of a lounge on the upper deck). The upward-opening SCD was 11ft wide by 10ft 6in high and the floor of Zone E was strengthened and equipped with cargo handling equipment, including a ball transfer unit in the entrance and roller tracks to facilitate positioning of the pallets once they were aboard.

Although, in Sabena's case, the passenger-cargo combination proved useful during the two economically difficult years that followed the modification of the aircraft, it created a problem during summer months when there was a need to operate all-passenger flights as additional services on scheduled routes and as charters. This meant a time-consuming conversion job and, to overcome this problem. Sabena's engineering department developed a **Quick-Change** procedure for the 747's Zone E based on the procedures used in its Boeing 727QC and 737QC. With this procedure, the cargo handling equipment is left in position on the floor and 12 rows of mainly ten-abreast seats, mounted on eight pallets (complete with carpets and power connections) are loaded aboard and locked in position. This raises the height of the floor in Zone E by about 8in. but the step is eliminated by using carpeted ramps. With this procedure, the rear galley (of reduced size), rear toilets, cabin trim and drop ceiling remain on board when the zone is used for cargo, to reduce the amount of change required, and it only remains to fit the overhead stowage bins to complete the conversion. Before the introduction of this procedure, it took days to convert Zone E from one mode to another, but with the quick-change procedure Sabena claimed that six men could do the job in 75min.

Only one 747-200F (No.168 for Lufthansa) had been built during the first five years of 747 production but in 1974 the air cargo market began to turn towards bigger aircraft and the second Freighter (No.242) was rolled out in June 1974 as N701SW for Seaboard World, the first **747-200F with SCD**. This aircraft was similar to Lufthansa's Freighter but in addition to the nose door it also had the optional side cargo door so that items of cargo as high as 10ft could be accepted. Because of the upper-deck floor, loads entering the cargo compartment through the nose opening are limited to just over 8ft high but once past the 'hump' the height of the compartment increases and the SCD provides access to this area. Containers with lengths of up to 20ft can be loaded through this door, allowing a certain amount of load changing at either end of the compartment at intermediate stops along a route. The Seaboard World Freighters were given the general name of *Containership*, and on the airline's trans-Atlantic cargo services emphasis was placed on the use of 'intermodal' containers which could be 20, 30 or 40ft long and were suitable for transfer from one mode of transport to another (air/road/rail/sea) so that container contents did not have to be removed from one type of container and repacked into another at points of transfer.

This first 747-200F for Seaboard World was initially delivered with a maximum take-off weight of 785,000lb because it was powered by Pratt & Whitney JT9D-7 engines but, when the JT9D-70A engines became available in 1975, it was returned to the factory for conversion to these later engines so that its maximum take-off weight could be increased to 820,000lb, to match the airline's second aircraft (No.266) which was delivered to this standard. Apart from the SCD, the Seaboard World Freighter also differed from the Lufthansa aircraft in having windows in the upper deck compartment, and an extra emergency exit door on the left-hand side behind the flight deck; these features were to prove useful a few years later when the airline started carrying passengers up there on its trans-Atlantic cargo services between New York and Frankfurt.

During the period **July to December 1974**, eleven 747s were rolled out (Nos.243 to 253), being three 747-100s (additional aircraft for British Airways and Air France), five 747-200Bs (additional aircraft for CP Air, JAL and Singapore), two 747-200Fs (the first Freighters for JAL and Air France), and the first 747-200B Combi (No.250) for Air Canada.

The JAL and Air France Freighters (Nos.243 and 245) were similar to the Seaboard World aircraft, with nose and side cargo doors and a maximum take-off weight of 785,000lb, but were both powered by Pratt & Whitney JT9D-7AW engines.

Although the two Sabena 747-100s had been modified earlier in the year to have the side cargo door, and therefore were the first 747s with the Combi configuration (combined passenger and cargo), the first 747 to be built as a **747-200B Combi** was No.250 (C-GAGA for Air Canada), which also became the 250th 747 to be delivered. This variant is basically a 747-200B with an optional side cargo door and strengthened floor (with cargo handling equipment) to accommodate cargo in Zones D and E of the main cabin. The arrangement suits airlines with seasonal fluctuations in passenger and cargo demands, and a typical application could have the aircraft with an all-passenger configuration during summer months, with passengers plus cargo in Zone E (six pallets) during spring and autumn, and with passengers plus cargo in Zones D and E (12 pallets or five 20ft containers and two 10ft containers) during winter. Other applications include the use of the aircraft in a combined passenger and cargo configuration all-year round on routes where neither passenger traffic nor cargo flow alone could support a separate service; this application is good for both because it provides wide-body comfort for passengers and regular container shipments on scheduled passenger services for cargo agents. With cargo only in Zone E, a 747-200B Combi has about the same capacity as one wide-body tri-jet (DC-10 or L-1011) passenger aircraft and one 707/DC-8 Freighter combined.

A divider wall, which separates the cargo in the rear from the normal passenger cabin in the front, can have the same decor as the remainder of the cabin so that passengers entering the aircraft through the usual doorways at the front will probably not realise that there is a cargo compartment behind them. Loading and unloading of both passengers and cargo can be performed simultaneously so that no extra time is required for turn-rounds at intermediate stops.

Typical conversion times quoted by Boeing, when employing an experienced 16-man crew and confining the conversion to an 8ft ceiling, are 8hr for all-passenger to six pallets in Zone E or 14hr for all-passenger to 12 pallets in Zones

The 747-200B Combi can accommodate various loads, ranging from all-passenger to passengers in Zones A, B and C and cargo in Zones D and E. (Lufthansa)

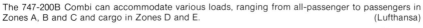

D and E, or 6hr to extend the cargo compartment from Zone E to Zones D and E; the reverse conversions take slightly longer and are 8hr to reduce the cargo compartment from Zones D and E to Zone E, 18hr for 12 pallets in Zones D and E to all-passenger, and 10hr for six pallets in Zone E to all-passenger.

Passenger accommodation in the 747-200B Combi can be arranged to suit an individual airline's requirements within the limits of the zones available. Typical mixed-class totals, with 28 first-class passengers and ten-abreast seating for economy zones in each layout, are 439 all-passenger, 303 with cargo in Zone E and 225 with cargo in Zones D and E. In all three layouts, the first-class passengers occupy Zone A, and the upper-deck compartment is given over to 32 economy-class passengers (seated six abreast with central aisle).

The 32-seat upper deck compartment became available as an option on aircraft built from July 1974 onwards, provided that an additional door was fitted on the left-hand side of the upper deck and that both this and the existing right-hand door were equipped with a special inflatable slide to serve as emergency exits. These slides were approved by the FAA in mid-1975 together with other changes to the emergency equipment, including the introduction of combined inflatable slides and life rafts which are stowed on the inside of the entrance doors and replaced the separate slides and inflatable life rafts previously carried (the life rafts in earlier aircraft were stowed in the ceiling of the passenger cabin).

Another variant equipped with a side cargo door is the **747-100SF**, which is the unofficial (but commonly used) designation for a 747-100 passenger aircraft which has been converted into a freighter by the addition of a SCD. This was another result of the oil price crisis in 1974 when some 747s were withdrawn from service and became surplus to an airline's requirements. Flying Tiger Line (an American domestic and trans-Pacific cargo carrier) started the fashion when it bought two 747-100s of American Airlines, which had been sold back to Boeing, who converted the aircraft (at its Wichita, Kansas plant) by stripping out the passenger interior, strengthening the main deck, covering the windows, sealing all doors except Nos.1 and 5 on the left-hand side, installing a side cargo door and equipping the interior with a cargo handling system. This conversion job took two to three months. While the aircraft were being converted, Pratt & Whitney were converting the engines from JT9D-3A to JT9D-7A standard. When the aircraft were delivered in August and September 1974 they were cleared for an increased take-off weight of 733,000lb which enabled them to carry a payload of 222,000lb on domestic routes and 215,000lb on international routes. Flying Tigers paid $22½ million for each aircraft, including the modifications and upgrading of the engines, which was about $10 million less than a new 747-200F at the time.

Flying Tigers later purchased four more 747-100SFs from Boeing (one ex-American and three ex-Delta) and American Airlines followed suit by having four of its remaining 747-100s converted to 747-100SFs. Both operators were concentrating on the use of 10ft long containers and palletised loads so that the container-length restriction of the side cargo door was not a problem, and the smaller payload of the 747-100SF was adequate for their operations.

The 747 suffered its first fatal accident in November 1974 when Lufthansa's D-ABYB crashed on take-off at Nairobi because the leading-edge flaps had not been properly extended. Of the 140 passengers and 17 crew aboard, 55 passengers and 4 crew were killed.

However 1974 ended on a happier note when the size of the 747 proved so useful in the evacuation of the Australian city of Darwin which had been hit by a cyclone called Tracey early on Christmas Day. In four days the Royal Australian Air Force and the Australian airlines flew 23,500 people to Sydney, Melbourne and Adelaide, and created some world records in the process. On December 28, a Qantas 747 took off with 633 passengers, followed by another carrying 634 passengers. And on December 29, a Qantas 747 set a world record by carrying 674 passengers, comprising 306 adults, 328 children and 40 babies. These high passenger loads were achieved by asking every adult with uninjured arms and legs to nurse a child. Other children were placed two to a seat, and some babies were placed on the floor between passengers' legs. The baggage allowance for each passenger was strictly limited, but in many cases the victims had little or nothing to take with them.

A 747 variant with a marked change in external appearance was rolled out with suitable ceremony on May 19, 1975. This was the first **747SP (Special Performance)** – No.265 (N530PA for Pan Am). With a fuselage 48ft shorter than all existing 747s, the 747SP was easily recognisable. Because of the considerable difference between the 747SP and other 747s, which is both technical and operational, a separate section following this one is devoted entirely to this variant so that it can be treated in more detail.

The 14 747s rolled out during the period **January to June 1975** were Nos.254 to 266 and No.268, the break in sequence occurring because the second assembly line was re-started to assemble the 747SPs, with No.265 being the first off and No.268 (N531PA for Pan Am) the second. The other 747s rolled out were one 747-100 (an additional aircraft for JAL), three 747-200Bs (additional aircraft for JAL, TAP and Qantas), three 747-200Fs (the second aircraft for Seaboard World and the first two Freighters for Northwest), one 747-100SR (an additional aircraft for JAL), three 747-200B Combis (first aircraft for Middle East Airlines) and the first E4B for the US Air Force.

At the time of roll-out, the E4B had an external appearance similar to the third E4A, being powered by General Electric CF6-50E engines, but its internal equipment was to be significantly different, as described later in the 747 Operators section.

The Qantas 747-200B (No.260 – VH-EBJ) was the first to be powered by Pratt & Whitney JT9D-7F engines, which were rated at 48,000lb thrust, dry, or 50,000lb thrust with water injection. This increase in power enabled a further increase in maximum take-off weight to be made, to 800,000lb, and the aircraft was also equipped with optional US800gal extended range tanks in the outer wings which, with some small changes in the existing tanks, increased the total fuel capacity to US53,160gal. Weighing over 355,000lb, the fuel load on a 747 was now greater than the maximum take-off weight of a 707.

As mentioned previously, the second Freighter for Seaboard World (No.266 – N702SW) was the first to be powered by Pratt & Whitney JT9D-70A engines, which were rated at 53,000lb thrust. When certificated in April 1976, these more powerful engines enabled the maximum take-off weight to be further increased to 820,000lb.

Of the eleven 747s rolled out between **July and December 1975** (No.267 and Nos.269 to 278), four were 747SPs rolled out off the second assembly line – Nos.270 and 273 for Pan Am, and Nos.275 and 278, the first for Iran Air. Variants of standard length rolled out during this period were three 747-200Bs (additional aircraft for Qantas and Air India, and the first aircraft for Aerolineas Argentinas), one 747-200F (an additional aircraft for Northwest), one 747-200C (the first Convertible for El Al) and two 747-200B Combis (the first Combis for KLM).

The KLM 747-200B Combis (Nos.271 and 276 – PH-BUH and PH-BUI, respectively) were the first civil 747s to be powered by General Electric CF6-50E engines (52,500lb thrust) and had the increased maximum take-off weight of 800,000lb. These aircraft also incorporated several optional features first introduced for the 747SP (and described in the next section), including a longitudinal galley in Zone B and an upper-deck compartment with contoured ceiling panels and improved soundproofing and seating for 32 economy-class passengers who have their meals sent up on food-cart elevators to a galley at the rear. Also, the cargo compartment in Zones D and E has a powered cargo handling system to reduce the time taken to load and unload. Total passenger capacity is 208, including the 32 in the upper-deck compartment and 20 first-class in Zone A.

In October 1975, Boeing announced that 100 million passengers had been carried in 747s world-wide.

By a strange coincidence two 747s were badly damaged in separate accidents in December 1975 and both were considered to be insurance write-offs after initial inspection but, thanks to the efforts of a team of Boeing engineers (who at times worked under very difficult conditions) they were restored to full health again in 1976. The first aircraft was an ex-American Airlines 747-100SF being operated by Trans Mediterranean Airways (OD-AGC) on a non-scheduled freight flight from Beirut to Athens on December 3, which over-ran a wet runway on landing and ended up in a wide ditch. The nose landing gear was pushed up into the nose section and the right-hand wing gear collapsed into the inboard trailing-edge flaps. The other landing gears sank into mud resulting in severe damage to the engines and lower fuselage. Moving an aircraft of this size and weight when it is lying on its belly in the mud is no easy task but they managed it and transferred the 747 to an open site alongside the Olympic Airways' hangars. The Boeing team worked on the aircraft from the beginning of February to March 20, renewing sections of the aircraft's underside, repairing damage to wings and engine pylons, and generally restoring it to its original state. And the aircraft was back on its scheduled service between Beirut and New York at the beginning of April after its $10 million restoration.

The second accident involved a 747-200B of Japan Air lines (JA8122) which was blown off an ice-covered taxiway by strong cross-winds while preparing to leave Anchorage, Alaska, on a scheduled passenger service from London to Tokyo on December 16. The aircraft suffered rather more damage than the TMA aircraft because it slid backwards down a 50ft snow-covered embankment and came to rest straddling a gulley. Once again a major problem was moving such a large and heavy aircraft without causing more damage to it, and an access road had to be built and three heavy cranes, plus airbags under the wings, were used to lift the aircraft so that the landing gear could be repaired sufficiently for the aircraft to be towed. As at Athens, no hangar space was available so an open site was used for the round-the-clock repair job which had to be completed during the arctic summer; floodlighting was installed although this was only needed during the two hours or so of darkness each day. The whole of the underside of the fuselage from the cabin floor downwards was badly damaged and was renewed completely, with the components for the replacement sections being produced by the usual sub-contractors, transferred to Everett for assembly on production jigs and then taken by ship to Anchorage. Nearly 500,000lb of material (fuselage sections, parts and tools) had to be shipped to Alaska and was on site when the Boeing team started work in mid-June. At the peak of the operation Boeing had over 100 people working on the aircraft and, typical of the company, the job was completed on time, with the aircraft having a test flight in the hands of a Boeing crew on August 29. After a further test flight by a JAL crew, the aircraft was flown to Japan for re-painting and interior refurbishing. Then, almost as good as new except for a slight weight increase, JA8122 was returned to service at the beginning of October 1976. The total cost of this restoration was around $21 million which was still considerably less than the price of a new 747-200B which by then was over $30 million.

Advance-purchase excursion (Apex) fares were introduced by IATA airlines on the North Atlantic route in April 1975. These were the scheduled airlines' answer to the advance-booking charters (ABC) being provided by air charter operators and offered passengers a cheaper flight provided they booked it at least 60 days in advance and confined the stay at their destination to between 14 and 45 days. These lower fares, together with inclusive-tour excursions (ITX) covering package holidays, proved very popular and started another change in the 747 passenger cabins because, to achieve the same revenue from these lower-yield fares, many scheduled airlines introduced ten-abreast seating (arranged 3 x 4 x 3). As with the introduction of tourist/economy class originally, this was a matter of comfort versus cost and passengers got the cheaper fares for a reduction in comfort, because to fit ten seats across the cabin meant using narrower seats and reducing the width of the aisles. Singapore Airlines was first to make the change, followed by British Airways, Pan Am had earlier introduced ten-abreast seating on its 747s operating between New York and San Juan (Puerto Rico) and extended the change later. Singapore Airlines also introduced a three-class cabin at the same time, by allocating seats in Zone C to full-fare economy-class passengers (usually businessmen) and giving them extra attention from the cabin staff – an idea copied by other airlines later.

Of the 13 747s rolled out between **January and June 1976** (Nos.279 to 291), two were 747-100s (additional aircraft for Air France and British Airways), two were 747-200Bs (additional aircraft for Singapore and Qantas), two were 747-200Cs (the first aircraft for Iraqi Airways), one was a 747-200B Combi (the first Combi for Iran Air) and six were 747SPs (the fourth SP for Pan Am, the first three SPs for South African and the first two aircraft for Syrianair).

The 747-100 for British Airways (No.281 – G-BDPV) was the last of the basic 747-100s to be built, and as an indication of the development the variant had undergone during the preceding six years, this had JT9D-7 engines, a maximum take-off weight of 735,000lb and an extended upper-deck compartment which had ten windows on each side, an extra door on the left-hand side and seating for 32 economy-class passengers.

An unusual feature of the two 747-200Cs for Iraqi Airways (Nos.287 and 289 – YI-AGN and YI-AGO, respectively) was that they were the first of the variant to be fitted with a side cargo door and also the first 747s to be equipped with an on-board loader. Stowed in Zone A and deployed through the nose-door opening, the on-board loader can be used to load containers or pallets into Zones D and E through the side cargo door opening or simply load and accommodate one 20ft container, or two 10ft containers or three pallets in Zone A. The equipment can be powered by the aircraft's auxiliary power unit, enabling the aircraft to be completely self-contained at airports not equipped for cargo handling.

During the period **July to December 1976** ten 747s were rolled out (Nos.292 to 301), comprising one 747-200B (the first 747-200B for British Airways), one 747-200F (an additional Freighter for Air France), five 747-200B Combis (an additional aircraft for Iran Air, the first two Combis for Lufthansa and the first aircraft for Alia, the Royal Jordanian Airline), and three 747SPs (additional aircraft for South African).

The 747-200B for British Airways (No.292 – G-BDXA) was the first 747 to be powered by Rolls-Royce RB211-524B engines of 50,000lb thrust and went on to do the certification tests for this airframe/engine combination with an eventual take-off weight of 820,000lb. In fact it did more than that, because on November 1, 1976 it set a new world record by taking off at a weight of 840,500lb, beating the 747's own record of 820,700lb set in November 1970.

Iran Air's second 747-200B Combi (EP-IAH) rolled out on December 2, 1976 was the **300th 747** to be completed.

Of the nine 747s rolled out between **January and June 1977** (Nos.302 to 310), four were 747-200Bs (two additional RB211-powered aircraft for British Airways and additional aircraft for Qantas and Singapore), one 747-200F (an additional Freighter for Northwest), one 747-200B Combi (the first Combi for Air France), and three 747SPs (additional aircraft for Pan Am and Iran Air, and the first 747SP for China Airlines).

What is likely to be recorded as the most unusual payload for a 747 was carried in February 1977 when a 747 took off with a space shuttle Orbiter on its back at the start of a test programme to enable the Orbiter to be air launched so that its handling and landing characteristics could be checked. The aircraft was an ex-American Airlines 747-100 owned by the National Aeronautics and Space Administration (N905NA) and modified by Boeing to have a strengthened fuselage with hefty support struts for the Orbiter and large end-plate fins on the tips of the tailplane, which were necessary to restore directional stability lost with the Orbiter mounted in front of the 747's fin. The combined weight of the two aircraft at take-off was 584,000lb and the 747 was powered by JT9D-7H engines (JT9D-3As modified to produce 46,950lb thrust) to improve performance. Further details of these tests and subsequent operations of NASA's 747 are given in the 747 Operators section.

Only seven 747s were rolled out during the period **July to December 1977**, the lowest figure for a six-month period since production had begun, but the tide was to turn again in 1978, and reach full flood once more in 1979. Of the seven (Nos.311 to 317), three were 747-200Bs (an additional RB211-powered 747-200B for British Airways, and additional aircraft for Qantas and Singapore), one 747-200F (the first new Freighter for the Imperial Iranian Air Force), and three 747-200B Combis (the second Combi for Air France, and the first Combis for SAS and Qantas).

The 747-200F for the Imperial Iranian Air Force (No.315 – 5-8113) was the first **Military Freighter** version of the 747 to be built and was similar to the nose-loading civil Freighters except for military avionics and other special equipment, with power provided by JT9D-7FW engines. The IIAF had previously purchased 12 ex-Continental and TWA passenger aircraft (victims of the 1974 fuel crisis) and ten of these had been converted to 747-100SFs to carry aircraft spares and other cargo from the USA to Iran. Three of the 747s were further modified into tanker/freighters by the addition of extra fuel tanks in the underfloor cargo holds and a refuelling boom beneath the tail; trials with the boom had been conducted in 1972 with 747 No.1.

A further increase in fuel capacity became available during this period as an option for 747-200B, -200C and -200F variants, taking the total to US53,985gal for aircraft powered by JT9D-7A and 7F and RB211-524B engines, or US53,611gal for aircraft powered by JT9D-70A and CF6-50E engines, with the maximum take-off weights remaining within the range from 775,000 to 820,000lb.

During the period **January to June 1978** the production rate was increased to four a month and 16 747s were rolled out (Nos.318 to 333). Of these, seven were 747-200Bs (three more RB211-powered 747-200Bs for British Airways, two additional aircraft for Air India, and the first new aircraft for China Air Lines and Wardair), one was a 747-200F (an additional aircraft for the IIAF), one was a 747-200C (an additional aircraft for El Al), four were 747-200B Combis (additional Combis for Lufthansa and Air France, the first new aircraft for Air Gabon and the first aircraft for Kuwait Airways), and three were 747SPs (two additional 747SPs for Pan Am and the first aircraft for the Saudi Arabian Government).

The 747SP for the Saudi Arabian Government (No.329 – HZ-HM1) was the highlight of this period because this was the first **747 Biz-Jet**, being intended as

No. 329 747SP HZ-HM1 (Bob Durey)

the personal aircraft of King Khaled of Saudi Arabia.

Of the 22 747s rolled out between **July and December 1978** (Nos.334 to 355), six were 747-200Bs (additional aircraft for Lufthansa, Qantas and Aerolineas Argentinas), six were 747-200Fs (additional Freighters for Lufthansa, Air France and the IIAF, and the first aircraft for UTA and Cargolux), eight were 747-200B Combis (additional aircraft for Lufthansa, KLM, Air Canada and Kuwait, and the first aircraft for Royal Air Maroc and Air Madagascar), and two were 747-100B (with Short Range option) for All Nippon Airways.

The **747-100B** replaced the original 747-100 and incorporated a strengthened structure and landing gear, to allow higher maximum take-off weights up to 750,000lb, and modifications to permit the installation of optional engines. With the introduction of this variant, the 747SR (Short Range) became an option of it, requiring only heavy-duty wheels, tyres and brakes, and a modified cabin pressurisation controller, to suit it for short-range duties while retaining its long-range capabilities; for the Short Range (SR) role, the maximum take-off weight was 520,000lb and seating could be arranged for a maximum of 550 passengers. The All Nippon aircraft (Nos.346 and 351 – JA8133 and JA8134, respectively) were powered by the de-rated CF6-45A engines of 46,500lb thrust and had seating for 500 passengers in an all-economy arrangement – the first 747s to have seating for 500 passengers.

Boeing re-activated the second final assembly line at Everett at the end of 1978 and stepped up the production rate to meet a welcome increase in 747 orders; 83 were ordered in 1978. During the period **January to June 1979** 31 747s were rolled out (Nos.356 to 386), comprising 16 747-200Bs (additional aircraft for Air France, British Airways, Northwest, JAL, Korean, China and Wardair, the first 747-200B for Braniff and the first aircraft for Cathay Pacific), three 747-200Fs (an additional aircraft for JAL and the first Freighters for Pan Am and El Al), seven 747-200B Combis (additional aircraft for Lufthansa, Air France, KLM, SAS and Kuwait, and the first new aircraft for Avianca and Pakistan International Airlines), three 747SPs (additional aircraft for Pan Am and Iran Air), and two 747-100Bs (an additional aircraft with SR option for All Nippon, and the first 747-100B for Iran Air).

Northwest's 747-200B N622US (No.357) was the first 747 to be powered by JT9D-7Q engines of 53,000lb thrust and was used for the certification tests. This new engine variant followed hard on the heels of the 50,000lb thrust JT9D-7J which was certificated in February 1979 when fitted to 747 No.359 (Kuwait's 9K-ADC).

Iran Air's 747-100B (No.381 – EP-IAM) was the first true 747-100B to be built and was powered by JT9D-7F engines, one of the engine options for this basic variant.

The 747 production rate reached the incredible figure of seven a month again in July 1979. During the period **July to December 1979** 41 747s were rolled out (Nos.387 to 427). Of these, 21 were 747-200Bs (additional aircraft for Northwest, JAL, KLM, Air India, El Al, Qantas, Singapore and Aerolineas Argentinas, and the first aircraft for Thai International and Philippine Airlines); one was a 747-200C (the first aircraft for Transamerica Airlines – the new name for Trans International Airlines (TIA)); eight were 747-200Fs (additional aircraft for Pan Am, Air France, Seaboard World, Iranian Air Force and UTA, and the first new Freighters for Flying Tigers); two were 747-200B Combis (additional aircraft for KLM and Qantas); three were 747SPs (the first 747SPs for TWA and Braniff); and six were 747-100Bs with SR option (additional aircraft for All Nippon and the first for JAL).

A fifth new Freighter for the Iranian Air Force (5-8117) was the **400th 747** to be rolled out, on August 27, 1979.

In January 1980, on the tenth anniversary of the 747's first commercial service, Boeing was able to announce that some 420 747s had been delivered and were in service with 57 operators, flying to over 150 cities world-wide. The productivity of the 747, with its 300 to 500 seat capacity, had made possible either reduced fares or only small increases, in spite of high rates of inflation and tripling of fuel prices. Nearly 123,000 passengers were flying in 747s every day, and the total number of passengers carried was over 266 million.

Although the 747 had changed little in external appearance over the years, with the exception of the shorter 747SP, the latest aircraft incorporated many improvements and were being produced in seven basic variants ranging from the 747SR, which carried as many as 500 passengers on Japanese domestic services, to the very-long-range 747SP, which regularly flew the longest air routes in the world. In between, there were the 747-100B and 747-200B passenger aircraft, and the Combi, Convertible and Freighter. These had maximum take-off weights ranging from 520,000lb of the 747SR to 833,000lb of the heaviest versions of the main variants, with power provided by a wide range of engines from three manufacturers and delivering up to 53,000lb of thrust while offering greatly improved fuel economy.

All of these variants were included in the outstanding orders for 747s, which at the beginning of 1980 brought the total sales of the aircraft to over 500 and would keep the Everett assembly lines busy well into the 1980s.

And, of course, there was always the possibility of other variants being added to the range. One could be a Combi version of the 747SP while, at the other end of the scale, the planned increases in engine power and maximum take-off weight would provide the basis for a 'stretched' version. Under consideration was a version which would be some 25ft longer, with an extended upper deck, capable of accommodating 120 additional passengers; a future Super 747SR could therefore carry as many as 620 passengers in an all-economy configuration, with 70 of these in the upper-deck compartment. Studies made by Boeing indicated that there was no technological limit to future aircraft size, although practical limits such as airport terminal design would have to be considered.

Special Performer

The Special Performance version of the Boeing 747, the 747SP, differs considerably both technically and operationally from the standard 747. Intended to fill the gap in the Boeing jetliner range between the 707 and the 747, the 747SP is smaller and lighter than the standard aircraft and has a performance that enables it to fly faster, higher and further than any other wide-body airliner.

This very-long-range capability has been utilised by some airlines to open the world's longest non-stop air routes, reducing journey times between such cities as New York and Tokyo, London and Cape Town, Sydney and Los Angeles, and New York and Tehran, which are all over 6000 miles apart. Other airlines have been attracted by the lower operating costs of the 747SP and use the aircraft on shorter, low-density routes which do not warrant an airliner the size

At the roll-out ceremony on May 19, 1975 the first 747SP was joined by 747 No. 1 for comparison of sizes. (Boeing)

of a standard 747. Yet another application for the 747SP is on long-range routes that require a take-off from a 'hot and high' airport, that is, an airport which has high daytime temperatures and is located thousands of feet above sea level, where conditions would prevent a standard aircraft from taking off with a full load of fuel and payload.

The first details of the 747SP were given in August 1973 when Boeing announced that it was proceeding with a new variant which would have a shorter fuselage and carry about 100 fewer passengers but would have a range of nearly 6900 miles, would climb quicker to cruising altitudes which would be up to 6000ft higher and would cruise faster with a 20 per cent reduction in fuel consumption. Once again, Pan Am led the way, with an order for ten in September 1973. The cost of a 747SP was given as about \$27½ million, compared with about \$31 million for a 747-200B.

Basically, the 747SP was a 747-100 with a shortened fuselage, but the removal of 48ft 5in of the fuselage required other changes and opportunity was taken to reduce weight wherever possible. Even shortening the fuselage was not a simple matter of removing a single section because portions had to be taken from both ahead of and behind the wing. To retain the same upper-deck compartment, it was necessary to modify the centre section of the fuselage, and a new rear fuselage section was required to provide a more abrupt reduction in fuselage width and lower the tail for aerodynamic reasons. To compensate for the shorter fuselage, the tip of the fin was extended 5ft and a double-hinged rudder was fitted in place of the single-hinged original. Because of the lowering of the tail, the increase in fin height results in an overall height increase of only 2ft and a difference in overall length of 47ft. The span of the tailplane was increased by 10ft by adding to the tips so that the main part of the tailplane and the elevators remained the same.

The wing box and centre section of the 747SP's wing are similar to those of the 747-100 except that it has been possible to save weight by reducing the gauge of the components because of the lower loads; the optional outer tanks are fitted as standard to allow the fuel capacity to be increased from 47,661 to US49,231gal when required. The trailing edges are completely new because, in place of the triple-slotted flaps, the 747SP has simplified single-slotted flaps which result in a considerable weight saving, and a reduction in drag because of the deletion of the big 'canoe' fairings covering the actuating mechanism of the original version. The basic engine for the 747SP is the 46,950lb thrust JT9D-7A but the engine attachments have been modified to permit the installation of other engines.

A maximum take-off weight of 660,000lb is standard for the 747SP, with an optional 690,000lb for an increased fuel load. Because of these lower weights, some landing gear components were redesigned to save weight but it is possible to interchange them with those of standard 747s.

Although these changes appear quite drastic, the 747SP still uses major parts of the standard 747 structure, or similar structure that can be built on the same jigs, and overall Boeing claims a 90 per cent commonality of components and parts likely to require changing by an airline.

The shortening of the fuselage, and the resultant reduction in the number of passengers, reduces the number of emergency exits required, and therefore the 747SP has only four doors on each side. The positioning of these doors has changed the interior of the aircraft somewhat, with the cabin now having only four zones, a similar size Zone A, a shorter Zone B, a larger Zone C and a similar size but tapering Zone D. Boeing took the opportunity when launching the 747SP of introducing some interior changes and additional options, which then became available also for customers of standard 747s. One of the problems with existing transverse galleys is that they are often used by passengers passing from one aisle to the other, which causes irritation to cabin staff during busy meal times, so to overcome this Boeing introduced a 16ft longitudinal galley on the right-hand side of Zone B, which can serve both first- and economy-class areas, and an aft galley at the rear of Zone D. These galleys provide private working areas for the cabin staff but reduce passenger amenities by displacing six-window seats in Zone B and four or six toilets in Zone D.

Further improvements were made to the upper-deck compartment by introducing illuminated and contoured ceilings, increased sound-proofing and separate air-conditioning controls. The 16 first-class (four abreast) or 32 economy-class (six abreast) seating was already available as an option on standard 747s, provided the additional left-hand door was fitted, but now an optional aft galley was available up there to cater for these passengers, supplies for it being provided by lift from the longitudinal galley on the main deck. For airlines with less concern for these passengers, or cabin-crew fatigue, the galley could be replaced by even more seats, making a total upstairs of 45, provided that a straight staircase was fitted in place of the spiral one to improve emergency evacuation. Where the upper-deck compartment is used as a passenger cabin instead of an in-flight lounge, provision can be made to show films so that these passengers can have the same facilities as those on the main deck.

From the pilot's viewpoint, Boeing aimed at providing the 747SP with handling qualities equal to or better than those of the standard 747, so that a 747 captain would require only a short conversion course to cover the differences. The flight deck of the 747SP is therefore similar to that of the standard aircraft, and the automatic flight control system required only minor changes.

To build the first 747SPs, Boeing re-activated the second final-assembly line at Everett, which had been closed when the production rate had been reduced in 1972. This allowed the 747SPs to be on the line for a longer period while experience was being gained in the assembly of the new variant. No separate batch of line numbers was allocated to the 747SPs so the first aircraft followed in the existing sequence and was 747 No.265. Again no prototype was built and this first aircraft was the first for Pan Am (N530PA) but for the roll-out ceremony on 19th May 1975 and the subsequent flight test programme the aircraft had a red, white and blue Boeing colour scheme; for its first flight on July 4, 1975 (in the hands of Jack Waddell) and flight test it had the special, and appropriate, registration N747SP. The next two 747SPs (Nos.268 and 270) were Pan Am's N531PA and N532PA and were painted in the airline's colours but for the flight test programme carried the registrations N247SP and N347SP, respectively. The fourth 747SP (No.273) was also for Pan Am (N533PA) but served as a back-up aircraft for the flight test programme and as a demonstration aircraft and so had a red, white and blue Boeing colour scheme similar to the first 747SP and was registered N40135.

During the seven-month flight test programme, the first three 747SPs logged a total of 544hr in 340 flights. Highlights of the programme included a speed of Mach 0.98 and operation at 46,000ft (the normal ceiling is 45,000ft); automatic landings to Category IIIA conditions were also included.

In addition, the fourth 747SP accumulated 140hr on a month-long, 72,000 mile, world-wide demonstration tour visiting 18 countries. Flown by Boeing crews headed by Jack Waddell and carrying Boeing personnel and representatives from various interested airlines picked up along the route, the aircraft first positioned from Boeing Field, Seattle, to New York, from where it set a record by flying 7015 miles non-stop to Tokyo in 13hr 33min. From there the tour continued to Taiwan, Singapore, Afghanistan (where Kabul airport is 5871ft above sea level), India and Australia. From Sydney, the 747SP made another long non-stop flight, this time 7143 miles across the Pacific to Santiago, Chile, in 12hr 14min. While in South America, the 747SP visited La Paz, Bolivia (which has the world's highest commercial airport at 13,354ft above sea level), Ecuador and Mexico. The airport at Mexico City is 7340ft above sea level and the 747SP took off at a weight of 631,000lb in a temperature of 75°F for its longest non-stop flight of the tour, 7205 miles across the Atlantic to Belgrade, Yugoslavia, which it reached in 12hr 56min. From here it flew on to Africa, via Greece, and visited Lusaka (Zambia), Nairobi (Kenya), where the airport is at 5327ft, and Abidjan (Ivory Coast) before returning across the Atlantic to Kingston (Jamaica) and Seattle.

When N40135 returned it was re-painted in Pan Am colours ready to become the first 747SP to be delivered, as N533PA *Clipper Freedom*, on March 5, 1976; this name was swopped soon after with that of N531PA/N247SP which had been *Clipper Liberty Bell* during the flight test programme. Incidentally, N533PA was the 2800th Boeing jetliner to be delivered.

The 747SP received its US Federal Aviation Administration type certification on February 4, 1976. At that time, 17 747SPs were on order for Pan Am, Iran Air, South African Airways, Syrianair and China Air Lines.

Pan Am was first to start 747SP services when it introduced the aircraft on new non-stop flights from Los Angeles to Tokyo (5478 miles) on April 25, 1976 and New York to Tokyo (6751 miles) the following day. By eliminating an en route stop on both services a saving of 3hr 45min was achieved, reducing journey times to 11hr 15min for the former and 13hr 45min for the latter.

The crewing of these very-long-range flights raised some problems because they exceeded normal working hours. If the aircraft had to carry a second complete flight crew and extra cabin staff, as well as having curtained-off rest areas in the main cabin (occupying revenue seats), the economics of the operation could be seriously affected. After discussions between the airline and the unions, it was agreed that an additional first officer would be carried and a rest area provided for cabin staff for use during quieter periods of the flight – plus overtime pay.

Iran Air, who started 747SP operations on May 1, 1976 on the Tehran-London-New York route, employed a normal flight crew when it introduced an eastbound New York-Tehran non-stop service in June (6121 miles in 11hr 15min), but the longer westbound flight against prevailing headwinds was not attempted, this continuing to stop at London en route.

South African Airways also started 747SP operations on May 1, 1976 but initially the aircraft were used on Johannesburg-Europe services alongside its 747-200Bs. However, the airline got into the very-long-range picture when its first 747SP (No.280 – ZS-SPA) set up a new world distance record for commercial aircraft when it flew 10,290 miles non-stop in 17hr 22min on its delivery flight from Everett to Cape Town on March 23/24, 1976.

Another 747SP spectacular took place in May 1976 when Pan Am's globe-trotting N533PA *Clipper Liberty Bell* made it "Around the World in 46 Hours". This special trip, arranged by Pan Am and carrying fare-paying passengers plus personnel from the airline and manufacturers, flew eastward from New York across the Atlantic to Delhi (for re-fuelling), then to Tokyo (for another refuelling), and finally across the Pacific back to New York. The flying time for the 22,864-mile trip totalled 39hr 26min, and the elapsed time, New York to New York (including a 2hr stop at Delhi and a 4hr stop at Tokyo) was 46hr 26min.

In normal airline service, passenger reaction to very-long-distance, non-stop flying was reported to be good, with most of them preferring to complete the journey as quickly as possible instead of taking a few hours more on one-stop or two-stop services. This was particularly so for businessmen who consider that the time saved en route can be used to better advantage at the destination recovering from any 'jet lag'. However, there were problems caused by spending long periods in a cabin with a pressure set to that existing at 8000ft. There were complaints of dehydration and, as on all flights of around 10hr or more, passengers were encouraged to take soft drinks frequently. Some passengers also had difficulty in breathing, and the addition of an extra circulation fan helped in this respect. Sufferers from bronchial and similar respiratory troubles would probably be advised by their doctor not to make such long flights.

Abnormal weather conditions during the winter of 1976/77 high-lighted another problem for high flyers in 747SPs: ozone irritation. The 'ozone season' occurs during late winter in the northern hemisphere and concentrations were unusually high that winter causing discomfort occasionally to passengers and crew. A charcoal filter, which absorbed up to 90 per cent of any ozone encountered, was installed in the air-conditioning ducts to overcome the problem.

To mark its 50th anniversary in October 1977, Pan Am renamed its 747SP N533PA *Clipper New Horizons* and took it on another round-the-world trip, this time flying 165 fare-paying passengers over both the North and South Poles.

Starting from San Francisco, it flew over the North Pole to London, then on to Cape Town, and finally over the South Pole to Auckland before returning to San Francisco. The elapsed time for this 26,706-mile trip was 54hr 7min (including the three refuelling stops) breaking the previous record of 62hr 27min set up in November 1965 by a specially-modified Flying Tiger Boeing 707.

In normal scheduled service, Pan Am 747SPs were operating the world's longest non-stop routes. In mileage, the longest route was the 7495 mile Los Angeles-Sydney route (which was flown non-stop only eastbound, taking 13hr 25min) but in flight time, the longest was the 7250 mile San Francisco-Hong Kong route which, westbound, had a flight time of 14hr 40min.

The 747SP did not prove as popular as Boeing had hoped and, with only 35 ordered at the end of 1979, the operators with them formed an exclusive club. Pan Am, Iran Air and South African were joined in June 1976 by Syrianair and in May 1977 by China Air Lines. Later, in October 1979, came Braniff and, in 1980, TWA and the Civil Aviation Administration of China (CAAC) of the People's Republic of China were due to join the club.

But top place in this exclusive club went to the 747SP ordered by the Saudi Arabian Government, which was equipped as a VIP aircraft and flying hospital for use by King Khaled of Saudi Arabia. This aircraft (747 No.329, suitably registered HZ-HM1) was also unusual in that it was the only 747SP powered by Rolls-Royce RB211 engines, all others being powered by Pratt & Whitney JT9D-7A, -7F or -7J engines. After its roll-out in May 1978, the aircraft spent over a year having a special interior fitted, and was delivered from Boeing in July 1979. This 747SP is likely to go into aviation history books as the largest and most expensive Biz-Jet in the world.

Big-Fan Engines

The high by-pass ratio turbo-fan engines which power Boeing 747s were developed from the by-pass engines and turbo-fans fitted to later versions of the first generation of long-range jet airliners, 707s, DC-8s and VC-10s. These engines were able to provide more power with considerably reduced fuel consumption, thereby improving the economics of jetliner operation.

Basically, the turbo-fan is a cross between a turbo-jet and a turbo-prop, with an enclosed fan at the front (replacing the propeller) producing a flow of air which is divided to provide a supercharged supply to a normal turbo-jet while the remainder is ducted around the outside of the engine (i.e. by-passes it). The difference between the amount of air by-passing the core engine (as the turbo-jet part is called) and the amount flowing into it is known as the by-pass ratio; on the early turbo-fans this figure was around 1.5:1.

The by-pass principle was conceived by Sir Frank Whittle in the early days of gas turbine aero-engines and was first put into practice by Britain's Metropolitan-Vickers with the Metrovick F.3 ducted-fan engine, which was a turbo-jet with a fan at the rear formed by having fan blades as extensions to one set of turbine blades. In this way some of the energy in the high-velocity gas stream was converted, via the turbine/fan, into a larger but slower-moving air stream. Greater propulsive efficiency is achieved when the ratio of the engine's jet velocity to the aircraft's flight speed is kept as low as possible, and the by-pass engine was developed to provide a power plant for aircraft with high subsonic speeds operating at high altitudes, whereas the turbo-jet is generally considered to be more suitable for supersonic aircraft and the turbo-prop (with its by-pass ratio of between 40:1 and 50:1) for lower subsonic speeds at lower altitudes.

General Electric (USA) converted its CJ-805 turbo-jet into an aft-fan engine, with a by-pass ratio of 1.5:1, to provide a suitable engine for the Convair CV990 in 1960; this conversion increased the thrust from 11,000lb to 16,000lb, and reduced the specific fuel consumption, for only small increases in frontal area, length and weight. A different approach to the by-pass principle was used in the Rolls-Royce Conway of the same period, which was a two-shaft engine with an oversize seven-stage low-pressure compressor, the excess delivery air from which was ducted around the outside of the engine; initially the by-pass ratio was 0.3:1 but was later increased to 0.6:1. The first engine to enter airline service with a fan at the front was the Pratt & Whitney JT3D, a modified version of the JT3 Turbo Wasp turbo-jet. The original JT3 was a two-shaft engine with a nine-stage low-pressure compressor driven by a two-stage l.p. turbine and a seven-stage high-pressure compressor driven by a single-stage

The size of a big-fan engine can be judged in this view of an inspector standing beside a CF6-50.
(General Electric)

h.p. turbine, and produced 11,000lb of thrust. To provide the by-pass airflow in the JT3D version, a 53in diameter two-stage fan replaced the first three stages of the low-pressure compressor, and a third l.p. turbine stage was added to provide the necessary increase in shaft power to drive the fan. The by-pass ratio was 1.4:1 and the fan airstream was discharged through a short-chord duct surrounding the front of the engine. The JT3D turbo-fan retained 90 per cent of the parts of the original JT3 turbo-jet but gave 52 per cent more take-off thrust with a 15 per cent better specific fuel consumption.

General Electric (USA) was first to develop big turbo-fans with high by-pass ratios, in which the by-pass airflow produces about 70 per cent of the thrust, and won the competition to power the US Air Force C-5A Galaxy transports with the TF-39 of 41,000lb thrust, the first of the big-fan engines, later to be developed into the civil CF6. Pratt & Whitney (with its JTF-14, later the JT9D) and Rolls-Royce (with its RB178, later the RB211) were close behind and by 1979 all three manufacturers were offering 747 customers a choice of these engines which have 8ft diameter fans, by-pass ratios of around 5:1 and thrust ratings of up to 53,000lb, with 60,000lb likely in the near future.

The Pratt & Whitney JT9D-1 of 41,000lb thrust was selected as the initial power plant for the 747-100. However, with the unexpected increase in

The JT9D-70A engines differ from other JT9Ds in having a long-chord fan cowling. (Seaboard World)

airframe weight in 1968, this version was restricted to use in the flight test programme and the more powerful JT9D-3 of 43,500lb thrust was made available for initial 747 deliveries. Early problems with this version were mainly overcome with the JT9D-3A which could produce 45,000lb of thrust with water injection at take-off.

Basically, the JT9D is a two-shaft engine, with the fan and a three-stage low-pressure compressor driven by a three-stage l.p. turbine on one shaft, and an 11-stage high-pressure compressor driven by a two-stage h.p. turbine on the other shaft. Internal modifications to increase pressures and operating temperatures led to a steady development of the JT9D, providing more power with reduced fuel consumption for later 747s, thereby increasing their range or payload. First was the JT9D-7 of 45,500lb thrust, or 47,900lb wet (i.e. with water injection at take-off), then in 1973 the -7A of 46,950lb thrust dry or 48,570lb wet, in 1975 the -7F of 48,000lb thrust dry or 50,000lb wet, and in 1979 the -7J of 50,000lb thrust dry.

To provide for future power increases, the JT9D underwent a major re-design to produce the 53,000lb thrust -70A in 1976. The fan diameter was increased by 1in, a fourth low-pressure compressor stage was added and a modified combustion system fitted. This version also had a change in external appearance, having a long-chord fan cowling in place of the familiar short-chord one; the only previous major external change had been the deletion of the 'blow-in' doors around the air intake to reduce noise. The long-chord cowling is called a 'common nacelle' because it is the same as that used for the JT9D in the DC-10-40 and A300. The most recent addition to the range in 1979 was the -7Q which was the same basic engine as the -70 but with a short-chord cowling for those airlines not requiring the common nacelle. The forthcoming -70B and -7Q1 produce 54,500lb of thrust and later versions of the planned -7R4 series will produce 56,000lb of thrust.

A second choice of engine manufacturer became available for 747 customers in 1974 with the General Electric (USA) CF6-50E of 52,500lb thrust. This engine had been developed from the 40,000lb thrust CF6-6 which entered airline service in 1971 powering DC-10-10s. The CF6-50E is a two-shaft engine which has a three-stage low-pressure compressor behind the fan and a 14-stage high-pressure compressor; after the annular combustion chamber there is a

The CF6-50 engines were fitted to 747 No. 1 in 1973 for certification trials on this airframe/engine combination.   (Boeing)

two-stage h.p. turbine and a four-stage l.p. turbine. It is basically the same as the CF6-50C engines which power the DC-10-30 and A300, and is fitted in a similar nacelle with a long-chord fan cowling. Future power increases include the CF6-80C of 56,000lb thrust.

The CF6-45A and -45B are the same as the CF6-50E but are de-rated to produce a lower thrust of 46,500lb to give them a longer in-service life. They are used in some 747SRs and are also suitable for 747-100Bs and 747SPs.

Rolls-Royce RB211-524B engines of 50,000lb thrust became available for 747 customers in 1977. They were developed from the 42,000lb thrust RB211-22 which entered airline service in 1972 powering the L-1011. The RB211 is unusual in that it is a three-shaft engine, and the -524 version has a fan driven by a three-stage low-pressure turbine on one shaft, a seven-stage intermediate-pressure compressor driven by a single-stage i.p. turbine on a second shaft, and a six-stage high-pressure compressor driven by a single-stage h.p. turbine on a third shaft. This arrangement results in a shorter engine, and the long-chord fan cowling extends to almost the full length of the engine.

By improving the cooling of the h.p. turbine blades, an increase in fuel flow was made possible, enabling the thrust to be increased to 51,000lb in the RB211-524C. A further increase to 53,000lb is planned for the RB211-524D.

Thrust reversal is provided on all big-fan engines, the rear of the fan cowling being slid rearwards to expose cascade vanes and the fan airstream deflected forward through these to provide reverse thrust during landing.

A cutaway view of an RB211 showing its internal arrangement, with the air intake and fan on the left. British Airways introduced the first of its RB211-524 powered 747-200Bs into service in July 1977.

(Rolls-Royce)

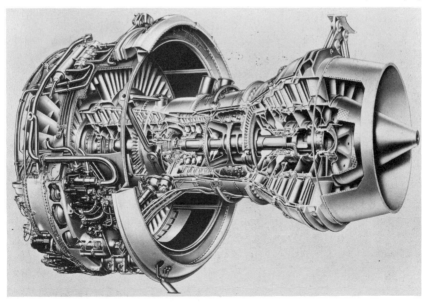

Operators are in chronological sequence. Abbreviations used in tabulated matter:

Reg'n	registration
WO	Written Off
Orig.	Originally
Cvtd.	Converted
Ret.	Returned
del.	delivered
SCD	Side Cargo Door
n.t.u.	not taken up
c/n	construction

BOEING – USA

Likely to be remembered in the years to come with as much affection as Dash Eighty, the 707 prototype, 747 No. 1 remained with Boeing, after serving in the initial flight test programme for 747 certification during 1969, to become a development and demonstration aircraft.

No. 1 747-121 N1352B City of Everett.   (Boeing)

By the tenth anniversary of its first flight, in February 1979, 747 No. 1 had accumulated 4500 flying hours testing equipment and modifications in a continuing product-improvement programme. Typical of this work was the testing in 1970 of the carriage of a spare engine beneath the left-hand wing, and in 1971 for the certification of the Category IIIA automatic landing equipment.

In 1972, 747 No. 1 was used to test the flight re-fuelling capability of the 747, under US Air Force sponsorship. For this the aircraft was equipped with a refuelling boom under the rear fuselage and made a number of dry contacts with various types of receiver aircraft, from fighters to B-52 bombers. The following year, 747 No. 1 was fitted with General Electric CF6-50 engines for the certification programme of this airframe/engine combination. Another job undertaken by the aircraft was to verify the control-system changes necessary for the 747SP.

Originally registered N7470, 747 No. 1 was re-registered N1352B in July 1970 and named *City of Everett*, but its colour scheme remained basically the same, with a white top, red cheat line and fin flash and blue titling.

Its next job is likely to be testing wing-tip extensions and active controls as part of NASA's Aircraft Energy Efficiency Programme to develop a version of the 747 with reduced fuel consumption during cruise.

PAN AMERICAN WORLD AIRWAYS – USA

The Clipper 747s of Pan Am need no introduction, having been in world-wide service since January 1970. Throughout the first ten years the airline maintained its lead position as the operator with the biggest fleet of 747s, a total of 47 having been delivered to it (comprising 100s, SPs, 100SFs and 200Fs), including two second-hand aircraft. As well as being the first airline to introduce the standard 747 into service, Pan Am was also the first to introduce the 747SP into service, operating them on the world's longest non-stop air routes.

In 1979, Pan Am's 747-100s were undergoing a refurbishing programme, and seating was being increased to accommodate 434 passengers, 29 first- and 405 economy-class. When required on certain routes, the first-class seating could be changed to Sleeperette seats and, as these require more space, 12 of the passengers are located in the upper-deck compartment, displacing the existing dining room. Sleeperette seats had already been fitted to the 747SPs which accommodated 264 passengers, 42 first- (14 upstairs) and 222 economy-class. The economy zones on all aircraft were divided into Clipper class at the front, for those paying full fare, and Economy class at the rear, for those paying reduced fares.

Trans-Atlantic cargo services were started in 1974 using a 747-200C leased from World Airways, but in the years that followed Pan Am formed a 747 cargo fleet of its own with four 100SFs (three passenger aircraft converted and one second-hand) which were joined in 1979 by two new 200Fs.

No. 268 747SP N531PA Clipper Freedom in later colour scheme. (Boeing)

FLEET

747-100 (Model 121A)

Line No.	Reg'n.	Delivery Date		Name (Prefix Clipper)	Remarks
2	N747PA	3 Oct	70	America	Leased to Air Zaire 73-75
3	N732PA	13 Jul	70	Storm King	
4	N731PA	11 Jul	70	Bostonian	Leased to Eastern 71-72
6	N733PA	12 Dec	69	Washington	Orig. Constitution
7	N734PA	19 Dec	69	Flying Cloud	
10	N735PA	9 Jan	70	Young America	Leased to Eastern70-72
11	N736PA	20 Jan	70	Victor	WO Tenerife 27 Mar 77
13	N737PA	21 Jan	70	Red Jacket	Leased to Eastern 71-72
14	N738PA	5 Feb	70	Defender	
15	N739PA	15 Feb	70	Morning Light	
16	N74OPA	24 Feb	70	Rival	Leased to American 70-71
17	N741PA	28 Feb	70	Kit Carson	
18	N742PA	2 Mar	70	Rainbow	
24	N743PA	28 Mar	70	Derby	Leased to American Mar-Oct 70
25	N744PA	21 Mar	70	Star of the Union	
26	N748PA	31 Mar	70	Hornet	
30	N749PA	10 Apr	70	Intrepid	

Line No.	Reg'n.	Delivery Date		Name (Prefix Clipper)	Remarks
32	N750PA	26 Apr	70	Rambler	
33	N751PA	24 Apr	70	Midnight Sun	
34	N752PA	2 May	70	Fortune	WO Cairo 7 Sept 70
37	N753PA	29 Apr	70	Westwind	
47	N754PA	26 May	70	Ocean Rover	
49	N755PA	31 May	70	Sovereign of the Seas	
50	N770PA	31 May	70	Bald Eagle	Orig. Great Republic
70	N771PA	4 Aug	70	Donald McKay	Cvtd to 121SF Apr 75
103	N652PA	25 Apr	71	Pacific Trader	
106	N653PA	8 Apr	71	Unity	
110	N654PA	27 Apr	71	White Wing	Cvtd to 121SF Mar 77
117	N655PA	28 May	71	Wild Fire	
127	N656PA	18 Jun	71	Live Yankee	
129	N657PA	19 Jun	71	Arctic	
131	N658PA	2 Jul	76	Fortune	Cvtd to 121SF Jun 76
142	N659PA	20 Dec	73	Plymouth Rock	

747SP (Model SP21)

Line No.	Reg'n.	Delivery Date		Name	Remarks
265	N530PA	26 Apr	76	Mayflower	
268	N531PA	17 May	76	Freedom	
270	N532PA	29 Mar	76	Constitution	
273	N533PA	5 Mar	76	New Horizons	Orig. Liberty Bell
286	N534PA	28 May	76	Great Republic	
306	N536PA	6 May	77	Lindbergh	
325	N537PA	9 Jun	78	High Flyer	
331	N538PA	12 Jul	78	Fleetwing	
367	N539PA	20 Apr	79	Black Hawk	
373	N540PA	11 May	79	White Falcon	

747-200F (Model 221F)

Line No.	Reg'n.	Delivery Date		Name	Remarks
384	N904PA	25 Jul	79	Bald Eagle	
392	N905PA	28 Aug	79	Golden Eagle	

Second-hand and Leased Aircraft

Line No.	Reg'n.	Delivery Date		Name	Remarks
46	N903PA	8 Jan	78	Express	Flying Tiger N800FT. Ret. Jul 79
72	N902PA	9 May	78	Mandarin	Model 132. Ex-China B-1868
143	N901PA	28 Jun	77	Carrier Dove	Model 123SF. Ex-TMA OD-AGC
209	N535PA	20 Oct	74	Mercury	World N747WA. Ret. Dec 79

TRANS WORLD AIRLINES – USA

TWA became the second operator of 747s in February 1970, first on the Los Angeles-New York route and starting trans-Atlantic services from New York to London the following month. The aircraft originally had the red arrowhead colour scheme but were being progressively repainted in the later red-tail scheme following its introduction in 1975. That year also saw a reduction in the size of the 747 fleet, when nine of the aircraft were sold to the Imperial Iranian Air Force, victims of the oil-price crisis, although one was bought back the following year. In 1979, the remaining aircraft had seating for 396 passengers, 33 of them in the first class who still had the use of an in-flight upstairs lounge, and 363 economy class with ten-abreast seating.

The airline became a member of the exclusive SP Club at the beginning of 1980 and the 747SPs were due to be on services between the USA and Europe, and possibly on longer non-stop flights from the USA to the Middle and Far East.

No. 9 747-131 N93103 in original colour scheme.   (TWA)

FLEET

747-100 (Model 131)

Line No.	Reg'n.	Delivery Date	Remarks
5	N93101	10 Aug 70	Sold to IIAF (5-280) Mar 75
8	N93102	31 Dec 69	Sold to IIAF (5-285) Nov 75
9	N93103	8 Jan 70	Sold to IIAF (5-287) Dec 75

Line No.	Reg'n.	Delivery Date	Remarks
20	N93104	20 Feb 70	
21	N93105	9 Mar 70	
28	N93106	3 Apr 70	
35	N93107	29 Apr 70	
38	N93108	7 May 70	
43	N93109	23 May 70	
63	N53110	10 Aug 70	
73	N53111	26 Sep 70	Sold to IIAF (5-283) Oct 75
78	N53112	4 Oct 70	Sold to IIAF (5-281) Mar 75
80	N93113	22 Oct 70	Sold to IIAF (5-282) Mar 75
85	N93114	2 Nov 70	Sold to IIAF (5-284) Nov 75
98	N93115	20 May 71	
102	N53116	22 May 71	
113	N93117	24 May 71	
151	N93118	2 Sept 71	Sold to IIAF (5-286) Nov 75
153	N93119	27 Oct 71	Sold to IIAF (5-288) Dec 75 Bought back 16 Dec 76

747SP (Model SP31)

Line No.	Reg'n.	Delivery Date	Remarks
415	N58201	Due Mar 80	
	N57202	Due Mar 80	
	N57203	Due Mar 80	

Second-hand Aircraft

Line No.	Reg'n.	Delivery Date	Remarks
76	N	Due Apr 80	Model 156. Ex-Iberia EC-BRO
91	N	Due Apr 81	Model 156. Ex-Iberia EC-BRP

LUFTHANSA – FEDERAL REPUBLIC OF GERMANY

The first European operator of the 747, Lufthansa introduced its first aircraft on the Frankfurt-New York route in April 1970, and the network was extended to the Far East and Johannesburg as more 747s were delivered. These early aircraft had seating for 361 passengers (including 28 first class with an upstairs lounge).

In April 1972, Lufthansa became the first airline to operate a 747 Freighter which it used on the Frankfurt-New York route, operating six round trips per week. Like the early passenger aircraft, the 200F was powered by JT9D engines.

The airline's first two CF6-50E-powered 200B Combis were delivered at the end of 1976 and were introduced on services to Australia and Los Angeles. In mid-1977 Lufthansa decided to change its entire 747 fleet to CF6-50E-powered versions, and the new aircraft (comprising four more Combis, three standard passenger aircraft and a Freighter) were delivered during 1978 and early 1979, the JT9D-powered aircraft being sold to Itel Air, an American aircraft leasing company. Lufthansa referred to the new aircraft as 747SLs (Super Long-

Range) but this was not a Boeing designation. With cargo in Zone E, the Combis carried 274 passengers (including 32 first class with an upstairs lounge). The standard aircraft, and Combis in all-passenger configuration, carried 404 passengers (including 32 first class with an upstairs lounge). All economy-class seating was ten-abreast, and three classes had been introduced on the trans-Atlantic route, the centre zones being economy/business class and the rear zone, tourist class. San Francisco, and Tokyo and Osaka via Anchorage, were added to the 747 network during 1979.

No. 347 747-230F D-ABYO. (Boeing)

FLEET

Original JT9D-powered Aircraft

Line No.	Reg'n.	Model	Delivery Date	Name	Remarks
12	D-ABYA	130	10 Mar 70	Nordrhein-Westfalen	Sold to Itel Nov 78 To Braniff (N610BN)
29	D-ABYB	130	13 Apr 70	Hessen	WO Nairobi 20 Nov 74
44	D-ABYC	130	23 May 70	Bayern	Sold to Itel Air Jan 79 To Aer Lingus (EI-BED)
132	D-ABYD	230B	5 May 71	Baden-Württemberg	Sold to Itel Air Nov 78 To Korean (HL7440)
168	D-ABYE	230F	9 Mar 72		Sold to Itel Air Dec 78 To Korean (HL7441)
179	D-ABYG	230B	25 Feb 72	Niedersachsen	Sold to Itel Air May 79 To Braniff (N611BN)

Later CF6-50E-powered Aircraft

Line No.	Reg'n.	Model	Delivery Date	Name	Remarks
294	D-ABYJ	230B Combi	23 Nov 76	Hessen	
299	D-ABYK	230B Combi	15 Dec 76	Rheinland-Pfalz	

Line No.	Reg'n.	Model	Delivery Date	Name	Remarks
320	D-ABYL	230B Combi	16 Mar 78	Saarland	
342	D-ABYM	230B Combi	20 Oct 78	Schleswig-Holstein	
345	D-ABYN	230B	10 Nov 78	Baden-Württemberg	
347	D-ABYO	230F	22 Nov 78		
348	D-ABYP	230B	7 Mar 79	Niedersachsen	
350	D-ABYQ	230B	13 Dec 78		
352	D-ABYR	230B Combi	11 Jan 79	Nordrhein-Westfalen	Leased to Condor until May 80
356	D-ABYS	230B Combi	8 Feb 79	Bayern	
	D-ABYT	230B Combi	Due Nov 80		

AIR FRANCE – FRANCE

Air France became the second European 747 operator in June 1970 when it started trans-Atlantic services from Paris to New York. During the 747's first ten years, the fleet was steadily increased to 25 aircraft, including some Freighters and Combis, and the 747 routes have been extended world-wide. All aircraft delivered since October 1976 were powered by CF6-50E engines and painted in the Concorde-style colour-scheme; earlier aircraft were later repainted in the new scheme.

Passenger accommodation on standard aircraft in 1979 was for a total of 381, with 32 in the first class and an upstairs lounge; when operated in an all-economy configuration the total was 437 with 16 upstairs. The Combis had cargo in Zone E and carried 281 passengers, 24 first class and 257 economy, including 30 in the upper-deck compartment. In the summer of 1979, Air France introduced a low-fare Vacances (Vacations) service between Paris and New York, and for this the standard aircraft had a 500-seat all-economy arrangement with 24 seats in the upper-deck compartment, ten-abreast at 33in pitch on the main deck, and no in-flight entertainment.

No. 22 747-128 F-BPVB in original colour scheme. (Air France)

FLEET

JT9D-powered Aircraft

Line No.	Reg'n.	Model	Delivery Date	Remarks
19	F-BPVA	128	20 Mar 70	
22	F-BPVB	128	25 Mar 70	
39	F-BPVC	128	12 May 70	
53	F-BPVD	128	14 Jul 70	
105	F-BPVE	128	16 Mar 71	
174	F-BPVF	128	4 Feb 72	
176	F-BPVG	128	2 Feb 72	
177	F-BPVH	128	1 Mar 72	
200	N28903	128	21 Feb 73	F-BPVI n.t.u.
201	N28888	128	30 Mar 73	F-BPVJ n.t.u. WO by fire on ground, Bombay 12 Jun 75
203	N28899	128	21 Feb 73	F-BPVK n.t.u.
224	F-BPVL	128	21 Mar 74	N88931 before del.
227	N63305	128	21 Dec 73	F-BPVM n.t.u.
228	N28366	128	8 Feb 74	F-BPVN n.t.u.
245	N18815	228F	4 Oct 74	F-BPVO n.t.u.
252	F-BPVP	128	13 Mar 75	
279	N40116	128	27 Feb 76	F-BPVQ n.t.u.

CF6-50E- powered Aircraft

Line No.	Reg'n.	Model	Delivery Date	Remarks
295	F-BPVR	228F	13 Oct 76	
303	F-BPVS	228B Combi	4 Apr 77	
313	F-BPVT	228B Combi	30 Sep 77	
333	N1252E	228B Combi	8 Aug 78	F-BPVU n.t.u.
334	F-BPVV	228F	9 Aug 78	
364	F-BPVX	228B Combi	28 Mar 79	
370	F-BPVY	228B	28 Apr 79	
398	F-BPVZ	228F	18 Sep 79	
428	F-GCBA	228B	Due Feb 80	
	F-	228F		

No. 303 747-228B Combi F-BPVS in later colour scheme. (Boeing)

BRITISH AIRWAYS – BRITAIN

The BOAC colour scheme was carried by the first 13 747s delivered to British Airways, the change of name and a new scheme being introduced in late 1973. Early aircraft were powered by JT9D engines but from 1977 all new aircraft delivered were powered by RB211 engines.

The airline's 747 services started on the London-New York route in April 1971 and were later extended to other trans-Atlantic routes and to Australia, the Far East and South Africa. The passenger total was progressively increased through the years, ten-abreast economy-class seating was introduced in 1975, and by 1979 the passenger total had reached 405 (29 in the first class with an upstairs lounge) or 435 all-economy with 32 in the upper-deck compartment. A Club class was introduced in 1978 for full-fare paying economy-class passengers, who were given seats in Zone C and provided with extra service. At the same time an Elizabethan Service was introduced on trans-Atlantic flights, providing first- and Club-class passengers with special meals and drinks of the period, and the theme was completed by naming ten of the aircraft after famous Elizabethans.

No. 23 747-136G-AWNA in BOAC's colour scheme.   (British Airways)

FLEET

747-100 (Model 136) with JT9D Engines

Line No.	Reg'n.	Delivery Date	Name	Remarks
23	G-AWNA	20 Apr 70	Sir Richard Grenville	
41	G-AWNB	22 May 70		
48	G-AWNC	29 Jun 70		
107	G-AWND	28 Feb 71	Christopher Marlowe	

Line No.	Reg'n.	Delivery Date	Name	Remarks
109	G-AWNE	5 Mar 71	Sir Francis Drake	
111	G-AWNF	14 Mar 71		
150	G-AWNG	8 Sep 71		
169	G-AWNH	23 Nov 71	Sir Walter Raleigh	
172	G-AWNI	7 Jan 72		
183	G-AWNJ	21 Mar 72	John Donne	
184	G-AWNK	24 Mar 72	William Shakespeare	
187	G-AWNL	19 Apr 72		
210	G-AWNM	3 May 73		
220	G-AWNN	7 Nov 73	Sebastian Cabot	
222	G-AWNO	7 Dec 73	Sir Francis Bacon	
246	G-AWNP	6 Nov 74	Sir John Hawkins	
248	G-BBPU	14 Mar 75	Henry Hudson	
281	G-BDPV	8 Apr 76		

747-200B and 200F (Model 236) with RB211 Engines

Line No.	Reg'n.	Delivery Date	Name	Remarks
292	G-BDXA	27 Jul 77		
302	G-BDXB	16 Jun 77		
305	G-BDXC	22 Jun 77		
317	G-BDXD	4 Apr 78		
321	G-BDXE	27 Mar 78		
323	G-BDXF	24 Apr 78		
328	G-BDXG	16 Jun 78		
365	G-BDXH	27 Mar 79		
430	G-BDXI	Due Mar 80		
	G-BDXJ	Due Apr 80		
	G-KILO	Due Sep 80		First 200F with RB211

Leased Aircraft

Line No.	Reg'n.	Delivery Date	Name	Remarks
108	G-BDPZ	1 Apr 76 to 28 Oct 78 and from 1 Apr 79		Leased from Aer Lingus (EI-ASJ)

No. 305 747-236B G-BDXC in British Airways' colour scheme.   (British Airways)

NORTHWEST ORIENT AIRLINES - USA

In keeping with its name, Northwest Orient's initial 747 services from July 1970 were across the Pacific from the airline's base at Minneapolis/St. Paul, plus Chicago, New York, Los Angeles and San Francisco, to Honolulu, Tokyo, Taipei and Hong Kong. However, in 1979 the airline added the trans-Atlantic route to its 747 network with services via New York or Boston to Glasgow (Prestwick), Copenhagen and Stockholm. In its advertising for the new routes Northwest was able to claim to be the 'The Roomy Wide-Cabin Airline' because the 747s still retained nine-abreast economy seating, the only change to the accommodation through the years being a reduction in first-class seating from 58 to 32 (who still had an upstairs lounge) allowing an increase in economy from 304 to 337.

The Northwest 747 fleet comprised a mix of 100s, 200Bs and 200Fs, the latest batch delivered in 1979 being powered by JT9D-7Q engines. Passenger aircraft had an unpainted top, a broad white and black cheat line and a red tail, while Freighters had only the red tail and titles.

FLEET

Line No.	Reg'n	Model	Delivery Date	Remarks
27	N601US	151	30 Apr 70	
40	N602US	151	12 May 70	
45	N603US	151	22 May 70	
55	N604US	151	24 Jun 70	
62	N605US	151	24 Jul 70	
71	N606US	151	30 Aug 70	
74	N607US	151	9 Sep 70	
75	N608US	151	18 Sep 70	
83	N609US	151	28 Oct 70	
88	N611US	251B	26 Mar 71	First 200B
93	N610US	151	11 Nov 70	
135	N612US	251B	16 May 71	
141	N613US	251B	22 Jun 71	
163	N614US	251B	22 Oct 71	
165	N615US	251B	23 Nov 71	
258	N616US	251F	3 Jul 75	
261	N617US	251F	9 Jul 75	
269	N618US	251F	29 Aug 75	
308	N619US	251F	27 Jun 77	
357	N622US	251B	24 Sep 79	First 200B with JT9D.7Q
374	N623US	251B	25 May 79	
377	N624US	251B	6 Jun 79	
378	N625US	251B	17 Jun 79	
379	N626US	251B	28 Jun 79	
412	N627US	251B	Due Jan 80	
	N628US	251B	Due Jun 80	
	N629US	251F	Due Aug 80	

Second-hand Aircraft

Line No.	Reg'n.	Model	Delivery Date	Remarks
68	N620US	135	May 76	Ex-National (N77772)
81	N621US	135	May 76	Ex-National (N77773)

JAPAN AIR LINES - JAPAN

The second biggest fleet of 747s at the end of 1979 was operated by Japan Air Lines, who had taken delivery of 34 aircraft during the 747's first ten years in service, comprising a mix of 100s, 200Bs, 200Fs and 747SRs.

Early 747 operations, from July 1970, were confined to trans-Pacific routes but these were extended to Europe in 1973. Domestic operations with the 747SRs also started in 1973, with the aircraft setting a record at the time by having seating for 498 passengers. By the end of 1979, the airline was considering a 550-seat configuration for these aircraft and an increase to 385 seats on its long-range 747s; the latter had been fitted with seven beds in the first-class upper-deck compartment.

FLEET

Line No.	Reg'n.	Model	Delivery Date	Remarks
31	JA8101	146	22 Apr 70	
51	JA8102	146	18 May 70	
54	JA8103	146	26 Jun 70	
116	JA8104	246B	11 Feb 71	
122	JA8105	246B	1 Mar 71	
137	JA8106	246B	14 May 71	
161	JA8107	146	28 Oct 71	Cvtd to 146SF Dec 77
166	JA8108	246B	30 Nov 71	
180	JA8109	246B	2 Mar 72	Blown up, Benghazi, 24 Jul 73
181	JA8110	246B	13 Mar 72	
182	JA8111	246B	21 Mar 72	
191	JA8112	146	14 Jun 72	
192	JA8113	246B	29 Jun 72	
196	JA8114	246B	3 Nov 72	
197	JA8115	146	4 Oct 72	
199	JA8116	146	8 Dec 72	
221	JA8117	SR46	26 Sep 73	First 747SR
229	JA8118	SR46	21 Dec 73	
230	JA8119	SR46	19 Feb 74	
231	JA8120	SR46	20 Feb 74	
234	JA8121	SR46	28 Mar 74	
235	JA8122	246B	29 Mar 74	
243	JA8123	246F	14 Sep 74	
249	JA8124	SR46	22 Nov 74	
251	JA8125	246B	17 Dec 74	
254	JA8126	SR46	2 Apr 75	
255	JA8127	246B	12 May 75	
259	JA8128	146	20 Jun 75	

Line No.	Reg'n.	Model	Delivery Date	Name	Remarks
361	JA8129	246B	6 Mar 79		
376	JA8130	246B	14 Jun 79		
380	JA8131	246B	28 Jun 79		
382	JA8132	246F	27 Jul 79		
407	JA8140	246B	8 Nov 79		
411	JA8141	246B	3 Dec 79		
426	JA8142	146B/SR	Due Feb 80		
427	JA8143	146B/SR	Due Feb 80		
432	JA8144	246F	Due Mar 80		
		246B	Due Dec 80		
		246F	Due Feb 81		
		246B	Due Mar 81		

ALITALIA – ITALY

Aviation pioneers and the first man on the moon, Neil Armstrong, are remembered by the names on the Alitalia 747s, the first of which entered service between Rome and New York in June 1970. In 1978 their seating capacity was increased to 416, and the following year Alitalia announced a 'roll-over' order in which nine new 747s powered by CF6-50E engines would be purchased to replace the original five.

FLEET

Original JT9D-powered Aircraft

Line No.	Reg'n.	Model	Delivery Date	Name	Remarks
36	I-DEMA	143	13 May 70	Neil Armstrong	
56	I-DEME	143	1 Jul 70	Arturo Ferrarin	To be
120	I-DEMO	243B	29 Mar 71	Francesco de Pinedo	sold
134	I-DEMU	243B	7 May 71	Geo Chavez	1981/82
190	I-DEMB	243B	26 May 72	Carlo del Prete	

Later CF6-50E-powered Aircraft

Model	Delivery Date
243B Combi	Due Nov 80
243B Combi	Due Dec 80
243B Combi	Due Dec 80
243B Combi	Due Aug 81
243B	Due Sep 81
243B	Due Nov 81
243B	Due Jan 82
243B Combi	Due Apr 82
243B	Due 82

CONTINENTAL AIRLINES – USA

The beautiful 747 Proud Birds of the Pacific, with their gold tails and gold and red cheat lines, were operated by Continental for only a short period from June 1970 to December 1973, when the fuel-price crisis caused their withdrawal.

They were operated on the Los Angeles-Honolulu route and at one time during the Spacious Age they had the lowest 747 seating capacity of all time with a total of 290 passengers arranged in three classes: 57 first, 145 coach and 88 economy who paid less but had no meals.

When withdrawn, the aircraft spent some time in the desert at Roswell, New Mexico, before going to new operators.

FLEET

Line No.	Reg'n.	Model	Delivery Date	Remarks
42	N26861	124	18 May 70	Sold to IIAF (5-289) Sep 75 and cvtd to 100SF Ret. to Boeing Jan 78 Then to World (N750WA)
58	N26862	124	13 Jul 70	Sold to IIAF (5-290) Oct 75 Ret. to Boeing Sep 76 Then to Avianca (HK-2000)
64	N26863	124	12 Aug 70	Sold to IIAF (5-291) Oct 75 and cvtd to 100SF Ret. to Boeing Apr 77 Then to El Al (4X-AXZ)
146	N26864	124	25 Jun 71	Sold to Wardair (C-FFUN) Dec 74

AMERICAN AIRLINES – USA

The unusual unpainted fuselage of American 747s, with only a red, white and blue cheat line and red titles (plus the red and blue AA on the tail) to provide the colour, came back into fashion in the late 1970s when some other airlines considered the weight-saving possibilities of such a scheme. American's 747 operations started in March 1970 on the New York-Los Angeles route using two aircraft leased from Pan Am until the first of its own 747s were delivered later in the year. These started operations with the general name of Astroliner but this was later changed to 747 Luxury Liner and for a period during the Spacious Age the aircraft really lived up to the name by having a piano bar at the rear of Zone E, which occupied the whole width of the aircraft, as well as a spacious interior generally.

As a result of the fuel-price crisis in early 1974, some of the original fleet of 16 aircraft were sold and others were converted into freighters so that the fleet in 1979 was eight 100s and three 100SFs, the latter usually operating US domestic freighter services but occasionally getting to Europe when leased to other airlines.

FLEET

All 747-100 (Model 123)

Line No.	Reg'n.	Delivery Date	Remarks
46	N9661	18 Jun 70	Sold to Boeing Feb 74 Then to Flying Tigers (N800FT)

Line No.	Reg'n.	Delivery Date	Remarks
57	N9662	16 Jul 70	Sold to Boeing Feb 74 Then to Flying Tigers (N801FT)
59	N9663	30 Jul 70	
65	N9664	27 Aug 70	
69	N9665	18 Sep 70	
77	N9666	2 Oct 70	Leased to Braniff Mar 78
79	N9667	8 Oct 70	
86	N9668	29 Oct 70	Sold to NASA (N905NA) Jul 74
87	N9669	27 Nov 70	
90	N9670	29 Dec 70	
115	N9671	26 Feb 71	Sold to Boeing Jul 75 Then to Flying Tigers (N802FT)
119	N9672	16 Apr 71	Cvtd to 100SF Jun 76
125	N9673	20 Apr 71	Cvtd to 100SF Oct 76
133	N9674	12 May 71	
136	N9675	25 May 71	Cvtd to 100SF Nov 74 Sold to TMA (OD-AGM) May 76 Bought back from TMA Jan 77
143	N9676	25 Jun 71	Cvtd to 100SF Nov 74 Sold to TMA (OD-AGC) May 75

Leased Aircraft

Line No.	Reg'n.	Delivery Date	Remarks
16	N740PA	25 Feb 70	Leased from Pan Am. Ret. May 71
24	N743PA	29 Mar 70	Leased from Pan Am. Ret. Oct 70

UNITED AIRLINES - USA

The biggest airline in the West, United Airlines had 18 747-100s in service in 1979 on its US domestic routes which included New York and Los Angeles to Honolulu, Hawaii, as well as coast-to-coast.

Operations started in July 1970, and in the early years the aircraft had lounges in the coach zones of the main deck but these were removed during 1973-74 to increase accommodation to 319, including 30 in the first class who had the use of an upstairs lounge. In the late 1970s the accommodation was further increased by introducing ten-abreast seating in the coach zones.

The exteriors of the aircraft had also undergone some changes, with the original red, white and blue scheme being first modified to a four-star Friendship version and then changed completely to a scheme which had a broad blue, red and orange cheat line and a red and blue 'U' on the tail. Some of the aircraft carried the names of executives of the airline, and one had the biggest 'name' given to any airliner - N4712U *The Original Eight* carried the names of the eight nurses who flew the San Francisco-Chicago route in May 1930, when hired by Boeing Air Transport (a predecessor of United Airlines) as the world's first airline stewardesses (Ellen Church joined first and the other girls were listed in their order of joining the airline).

FLEET

All aircraft are 747-100s (Model 122)

Line No.	Reg'n.	Delivery Date	Name
52	N4703U	30 Jun 70	William Allen
60	N4704U	7 Aug 70	
61	N4710U	8 Aug 70	
66	N4711U	28 Aug 70	Charles F. McErlean
67	N4712U	31 Aug 70	The Original Eight
89	N4713U	3 Nov 70	
97	N4714U	28 Nov 70	Justin Dart
99	N4716U	11 Dec 70	
101	N4717U	28 Dec 70	Edward E. Carlson
139	N4718U	27 May 71	Thomas F. Gleed
145	N4719U	26 Jun 71	
148	N4720U	23 Jul 71	
175	N4723U	6 Jan 72	William A. Patterson
193	N4727U	27 Jun 72	Robert E. Johnson
205	N4728U	27 Apr 73	Gardner Cowles
206	N4729U	24 Apr 73	
207	N4732U	19 Mar 73	
208	N4735U	30 May 73	

NATIONAL AIRLINES – USA

The Sun King symbol of sunny Florida formed part of the yellow and orange colour scheme of National's 747s and they were operated with the general name of Sun King when services started in October 1970 on the Miami-New York and Miami-Los Angeles routes. In May 1972 they were introduced for summers only on the Miami-London route and became well known as *Patricia* and *Linda* when they appeared in the airline's 'Fly Me' advertisements, all of National's aircraft carrying the names of stewardesses at the time.

Although victims of the 1973/74 fuel-price crisis, National's 747s continued in service until August 1975, when they were withdrawn and eventually sold.

FLEET

Both 747-100 (Model 135)

Line No.	Reg'n.	Delivery Date	Name	Remarks
68	N77772	8 Sep 70	Jacquelyn	Orig. named Patricia Withdrawn from service Aug 75 Sold to Northwest (N620US) May 76
81	N77773	20 Oct 70	Linda	Orig. named Elizabeth Withdrawn from service Aug 75 Sold to Northwest (N621US)|May 76

DELTA AIRLINES - USA

More victims of the 1973/74 fuel-price crisis were the five 747s of Delta, the first of which entered service in October 1970 on the Atlanta-Dallas-Los Angeles route. In their dark blue, white and red colour scheme, they became a familiar sight at London's Heathrow Airport between 1973 and 1975, operating a Pan Am interchange service on the Atlanta-Washington-London route.

By mid-1975 the fleet was down to three and, although these continued in service until 1977, they had already been earmarked for sale.

FLEET

All 747-100 (Model 132)

Line No.	Reg'n.	Delivery Date	Remarks
72	N9896	2 Oct 70	Sold to Boeing Sep 74 Then to China (B-1868)
82	N9897	22 Oct 70	Sold to Boeing Feb 77 Then to Flying Tigers (N803FT)
94	N9898	18 Nov 70	Sold to Boeing Mar 75 Then to China (B-1860)
155	N9899	30 Sep 71	Sold to Boeing Mar 77 Then to Flying Tigers (N804FT)
159	N9900	11 Nov 71	Sold to Boeing Apr 77 Then to Flying Tigers (N805FT)

IBERIA - SPAIN

Named after Spanish writers, the first three 747s of Iberia started life in a simple red and yellow colour scheme (the national colours) but to mark the change from republic to monarchy in 1977 an impressive new scheme was introduced as shown, using the same colours and with gold crown painted in the dot of the I of IB on the tail.

The 747s were introduced on the Madrid-New York route in December 1970 and were later also used on services to Canada and South America. The accommodation aboard was for 370 passengers, with 32 in the first class who had the use of an upstairs lounge. In 1979 Iberia ordered another 747-200B and planned to sell its two 747-100s to TWA.

FLEET

Line No.	Reg'n.	Model	Delivery Date	Name	Remarks
76	EC-BRO	156	2 Oct 70	Cervantes	Due to be sold to TWA Apr 80
91	EC-BRP	156	10 Nov 70	Lope de Vega	Due to be sold to TWA Apr 81
173	EC-BRQ	256B	4 Jan 72	Calderon de la Barca	
	EC-DIA	256B	Due May 80		

AER LINGUS - IRELAND

Originally wearing a green shamrock on a white tail when they entered service on the Dublin-New York route in April 1971, the Aer Lingus 747s later had a colour scheme reversal, ending up with a green top and a white shamrock. The aircraft spent some time leased out to other airlines but one was usually on the New York service in summer.

FLEET

Both 747-100 (Model 148)

Line No.	Reg'n.	Delivery Date	Name	Remarks
84	EI-ASI	15 Dec 70	St. Colmcille	Leased to Air Siam (HS-VGB) Sep 73-Apr 76. Re-named St. Patrick to fly Pope Rome-Dublin and Shannon-Boston Sep 79
108	EI-ASJ	18 Mar 71	St. Patrick	Leased to British A/W (G-BDPZ) Mar 76-/Oct 78 Leased to British Caledonian (G-BDPZ) Oct 78-Feb 79 Leased to British A/W (G-BDPZ) Apr 79-

Leased Aircraft

Line No.	Reg'n.	Delivery Date	Name	Remarks
44	EI-BED	5 Jan 79	St. Kieran	Leased from Itel Air (Ex-Lufthansa D-ABYC) Leased to Air Algerie Oct 79-

EASTERN AIR LINES - USA

Although the Eastern Air Lines' badge was among the customer airlines displayed on the nose of 747 No.1 when it was rolled out in September 1968, the airline's four assembly-line positions were sold to TWA before the aircraft were delivered. However, 747s did carry the airline's two-tone blue colour scheme for 16 months from January 1971 when Eastern leased aircraft from Pan Am and used them on the New York and Chicago to Miami routes in winter and from New York to San Juan in summer.

In 1979 Eastern was planning to use 747s on the Miami-London route if it was able to take over the route from National.

FLEET

Leased Aircraft
All 747-100 (Model 121)

Line No.	Reg'n.	Delivery Date	Remarks
4	N731PA	3 Jan 71	Leased from Pan Am in winters only, 1971 and 1971-72

Line No.	Reg'n.	Delivery Date	Remarks
10	N735PA	26 Nov 70	Leased from Pan Am. Ret. Apr 72
13	N737PA	1 Jan 71	Leased from Pan Am. Ret. May 72

SABENA – BELGIUM

Sabena's two 747s were standard passenger aircraft when they were introduced on the Brussels-New York route in Feburary 1971 but at the beginning of 1974 they were returned to Boeing to have a side cargo door fitted. This converted them into Combis, allowing cargo to be carried in Zone E and reducing the passenger total from 365 to 242, with 28 in first class who still had the use of an upstairs lounge. Later, to enable the aircraft to be operated in an all-passenger configuration, a quick-change procedure was developed to install 116 seats, mounted on pallets, in Zone E. In 1979, the passenger totals had been increased to 254 as a Combi and 370 all-passenger.

FLEET

Both 747-100 (Model 129)

Line No.	Reg'n.	Delivery Date	Remarks
92	OO-SGA	19 Nov 70	Cvtd. from passenger to Combi by Boeing Feb 74
95	OO-SGB	4 Dec 70	Cvtd. from passenger to Combi by Boeing Mar 74

KLM – NETHERLANDS

Named after the great rivers of the world, the first 747s of KLM entered service on the Amsterdam-New York route in February 1971, and later took over some other trans-Atlantic routes and services to Australia and the Far East. The first seven aircraft were powered by JT9D engines and had a white top colour scheme but this was later changed to a light-blue top scheme. A change to CF6-50E engines was made for aircraft delivered from 1975 onwards, which were mainly 200B Combis; these were named after aviation pioneers.

Passenger totals in 1979 ranged from 412 for an all-passenger, with 24 first class in Zone A and 388 economy class at ten-abreast and 32 in the upper-deck compartment, to 212 for a Combi with cargo in Zones D and E, 24 in the first class in Zone A and 188 economy class at ten-abreast and 32 upstairs.

FLEET

JT9D-powered Aircraft

Line No.	Reg'n.	Model	Delivery Date	Name	Remarks
96	PH-BUA	206B	16 Jan 71	Mississippi The Mississippi	
118	PH-BUB	206B	5 Mar 71	Donau The Danube	

Line No.	Reg'n.	Model	Delivery Date	Name	Remarks
138	PH-BUC	206B	21 May 71	Amazone The Amazon	
152	PH-BUD	206B	31 Aug 71	Nijl The Nile	
156	PH-BUE	206B	30 Sep 71	Rio de la Plata	Leased to Air Siam (HS-VGG) 1976-77
157	PH-BUF	206B	19 Oct 71	Rijn The Rhine	WO in ground collision, Tenerife 27 Mar 77
170	PH-BUG	206B	15 Dec 71	Orinoco	Leased to Viasa 1972-74

CF6-50-powered Aircraft

Line No.	Reg'n.	Model	Delivery Date	Name	Remarks
271	PH-BUH	206B Combi	19 Oct 75	Dr. Albert Plesman	
276	PH-BUI	206B Combi	15 Dec 75	Wilbur Wright	
336	PH-BUK	206B Combi	1 Sep 78	Louis Bleriot	
344	PH-BUL	206B Combi	4 Nov 78	Charles A. Lindbergh	
369	PH-BUM	206B Combi	15 May 79	Sir Charles E. Kingsford Smith	
389	PH-BUN	206B Combi	17 Aug 79	Anthony H.G. Fokker	
397	PH-BUO	206B	21 Sep 79	Missouri The Missouri	
	PH-BUP	206B	Due Sep 80	Ganges	
	PH-BUR	206B	Due Dec 80	Indus	
	PH-BUS	206B Combi	Due Oct 81	Admiral Richard E. Byrd	

BRANIFF INTERNATIONAL AIRWAYS - USA

The Big Orange went to (London) town in a big way in March 1978, at the start of Braniff's first trans-Atlantic service, but for eight years before that N601BN had been quietly trailing across the Pacific on its daily shuttle between Dallas/Fort Worth and Honolulu. By the end of 1979 there were seven Big Oranges, existing, new and leased aircraft, all carrying the bright orange colour scheme and operating services from Dallas/Forth Worth to Honolulu, London and (via Boston) Paris, Frankfurt, Amsterdam and Brussels; from Los Angeles to Honolulu, Guam, Hong Kong, Seoul, Singapore, Santiago and Buenos Aires; from New York to Buenos Aires; and from Miami to Santiago and Buenos Aires.

In October 1979 Braniff had joined the exclusive SP Club with the delivery of the first of its 747SPs, which were to be used mainly on its services to the Far East and South America.

Passenger totals varied but it was planned to standardise on 418 for standard 747s, with 32 in the first class including eight in the upper-deck compartment, and 301 for 747SPs, with the same arrangement for the first class.

FLEET
Standard Aircraft

Line No.	Reg'n.	Model	Delivery Date	Remarks
100	N601BN	127	5 Jan 71	100th 747 built
				Had flown over 40,000 hours by Dec 78
123	N602BN	127	—	Not delivered – traded in for 727s.
				Then to Wardair (CF-DJC) Apr 73
375	N602BN	227B	31 May 71	
	N605BN	227B	Due Apr 80	
	N607BN	227B	Due Oct 80	
	N609BN	227B	Due Apr 81	
	N612BN	227B	Due Oct 81	

747 SP

Line No.	Reg'n.	Model	Delivery Date	Remarks
405	N603BN	SP27	30 Oct 70	
413	N604BN	SP27	Due Apr 80	
	N606BN	SP27	Due May 80	
	N608BN	SP27	Due Sep 80|	

Leased Aircraft

Line No.	Reg'n.	Model	Delivery Date	Remarks
77	N9666	123	1 Mar 78	Leased from American (Orange cheat line only)
12	N610BN	130	29 Nov 78	Leased from Itel Air (Ex-Lufthansa D-ABYA)
179	N611BN	230B	11 May 79	Leased from Itel Air (Ex-Lufthansa D-ABYG)
237	N749WA	273C	10 Apr 79	Leased from World
244	N620BN	217B	15 Nov 78	Leased from CP Air (C-FCRD) Ret. Dec 78

AIR CANADA - CANADA

The maple-leaf symbol of Air Canada made its appearance on a 747 in April 1971 when the airline's first aircraft started services on the Vancouver-Toronto route, with Toronto-London services beginning in the June. The first six aircraft were delivered in the original red and white colour scheme which had black titles and an anti-dazzle panel on the nose, but a revised colour scheme was introduced in 1977 with a broader, wrap-around cheat line, titles and tail in a brighter red, and the black anti-dazzle panel was removed.

FLEET

Line No.	Reg'n.	Model	Delivery Date	Remarks
104	C-FTOA	133	11 Feb 71	Orig. CF-TOA
121	C-FTOB	133	18 Mar 71	Orig. CF-TOB

Line No.	Reg'n.	Model	Delivery Date	Remarks
144	C-FTOC	133	24 Jun 71	Orig. CF-TOC
214	C-FTOD	133	14 May 73	Orig. CF-TOD
236	C-FTOE	133	13 May 74	
250	C-GAGA	233B Combi	7 Mar 75	First 200B Combi 250th 747 delivered
355	C-GAGB	233B Combi	31 Jan 79	

SWISSAIR – SWITZERLAND

Swissair's two 747s were introduced on the airline's trans-Atlantic services from Geneva and Zurich to New York in April 1971 and through the years remained almost exclusively on those services, with the possible exception of the occasional charter elsewhere. And, most unusual in those times of capacity increases, the passenger total on these aircraft remained unchanged at 353, with 32 in the first class who had the use of an upstairs lounge, and 321 in economy class who were still only 9-abreast. A Swissair advertisement quoted a leading European newspaper which reported that 'Swissair is the only European airline committed to prevent the decline of in-flight comfort from sinking to the level of a sardine tin'. However, a colour-scheme change was due in 1980, with the red cheat line becoming black, and the black titles red.

FLEET

All 747-200B (Model 257B)

Line No.	Reg'n.	Delivery Date	Name
112	HB-IGA	29 Jan 71	Geneve
126	HB-IGB	25 Mar 71	Zurich
	HB-	Due Apr 82	

SCANDINAVIAN AIRLINES SYSTEM – DENMARK, NORWAY, AND SWEDEN

The Viking Fleet of SAS received its first 747 – SE-DDL, aptly named *Huge Viking* – in February 1971, and it was introduced on the Copenhagen-New York route in the April. A second 200B joined the fleet later that year and the 747 operations were gradually extended to include Chicago and Montreal on the other side of the Atlantic and Stockholm, Bergen, Gothenburg in Scandinavia. The first 200B Combi entered service on the trans-Atlantic routes in 1977 and the second Combi was introduced on the Copenhagen-Seattle-Los Angeles route in 1979.

SAS Combis were powered by JT9D-70A engines and had seating in summer for 281 passengers and in winter for 209, to allow cargo to be carried in Zone D as well as Zone E; in both cases there were 32 economy-class passengers in the upper deck compartment. By 1979, seating in the standard aircraft had been increased to 396, with 12 upstairs.

FLEET

Line No.	Reg'n.	Model	Delivery Date	Name
114	SE-DDL	283B	22 Feb 71	Huge Viking
167	OY-KHA	283B	12 Nov 71	Ivar Viking
311	LN-RNA	283B Combi	27 Oct 77	Magnus Viking
358	SE-DFZ	283B Combi	2 Mar 79	Knut Viking
		283B Combi	Due Oct 80	
		283B	Due Oct 81	

CONDOR FLUGDIENST – FEDERAL REPUBLIC OF GERMANY

The first airline to operate a 747 on non-scheduled services was Condor, the charter subsidiary of Lufthansa, who introduced its first aircraft in May 1971 on inclusive-tour holiday flights from various West German cities to resorts in Spain, Majorca and the Canary Islands; in winter it went further afield to find the sunshine and took its passengers to the Far East. The aircraft had an all economy-class layout for 470 passengers (the first 747 with ten-abreast seating), including eight upstairs, later increased to 16. A second aircraft was delivered in 1972 and operations were further extended. Although Condor referred to its aircraft by the names *Fritz* and *Max*, these were not painted on the aircraft.

Both aircraft were included in Lufthansa's roll-over re-equipment plan but Condor selected the DC-10 to replace them, and when they were sold in 1979 a Combi was leased from Lufthansa until the DC-10s were delivered.

FLEET

Line No.	Reg'n.	Model	Delivery Date	Name	Remarks
128	D-ABYF	230B	2 Apr 71	Fritz	Sold to Itel Air Jun 79 To Korean (HL-7447)
186	D-ABYH	230B	31 Mar 72	Max	Sold to Itel Air Feb 79 To Korean (HL-7442)
352	D-ABYR	230B Combi	11 Jan 79		Leased from Lufthansa Ret. due May 80

AIR INDIA – INDIA

'Your Palace in the Sky' was the inscription on the 747s of Air India and they had the stylish colour scheme and interior decor to suit. On the outside, each of the windows was treated individually in the red and white colour scheme, creating a palace-like appearance with a series of graceful Rajasthani-style arches. Appropriately, the aircraft were named after Emperors.

The interior of the aircraft was designed by Air India's art studio in Bombay and was inspired by the romantic folklore and legends of India. There were blue and pink panels in alternate zones of the passenger cabin depicting episodes from the life of Lord Krishna, one of the most revered Hindu Gods; and partitions dividing the cabin were decorated with wooden temple carvings and tapestries. Upstairs, the Maharajah Lounge was decorated with a large mural depicting the Ajanta cave frescoes, with scenes from the previous lives of Lord Buddah.

Air India's 747s were introduced on the Bombay-London-New York route in May 1971 and, at the time, had accommodation for 346 passengers, with 52 in the first class.

The first seven aircraft were powered by JT9D-7 engines but aircraft delivered from 1979 onwards were powered by JT9D-7Q engines.

FLEET

All 747-200B (Model 237B)

Line No.	Reg'n.	Delivery Date	Name (Prefix Emperor)	Remarks
124	VT-EBD	22 Mar 71	Ashoka	WO nr. Bombay 1 Jan 78
130	VT-EBE	20 Apr 71	Shahjehan	
185	VT-EBN	28 Mar 72	Rajendra Chola	
188	VT-EBO	1 Jun 72	Vikramaditya	
277	VT-EDU	23 Dec 75	Akbar	
318	VT-EFJ	3 Feb 78	Chandragupta	
330	VT-EFO	30 Jun 78	Kanishka	
390	VT-EFU	14 Aug 79	Krishna Deva	
414	VT-EGA	21 Dec 79		
431	VT-EGB	Due Mar 80		
434	VT-EGC	Due Mar 80		

EL AL –ISRAEL

El Al – Israel Airlines introduced its first 747 on the Tel Aviv-London-New York route in June 1971 and became the first scheduled airline to have an upper-deck comparment with saleable seats – this was arranged to accommodate eight first-class passengers and the whole of the main deck cabin was given over to 393 economy-class passengers. Later aircraft had the internally-extended upper deck, and the first aircraft was modified to this standard, so that the number of first-class passengers upstairs could be increased to ten. This arrangement was retained in 1978 when ten-abreast seating was introduced in the main deck cabin to increase the total seating to 437.

Through the years El Al had accumulated a mixed 747 fleet which, by the end of 1979, comprised four 200Bs, two 200Cs, one 200F and a second-hand 100SF. The 200Cs were for years the only ones of this 747 variant to be regularly converted from one role to the other each year. The airline had a peak in holiday passenger traffic in summer and required additional cargo capacity in winter, which was Israel's peak agricultural season, and the aircraft were converted to suit; when operating in the cargo role, the 200Cs usually had a 'Cargo' sticker behind the title. The 200Cs and 100SF were also at times leased to the Israeli cargo operator Cargo Air Lines (CAL) on short-term leases.

FLEET

Line No.	Reg'n.	Model	Delivery Date	Remarks
140	4X-AXA	258B	26 May 71	
164	4X-AXB	258B	22 Nov 71	
212	4X-AXC	258B	18 Apr 73	200th 747 del.
272	4X-AXD	258C	31 Dec 75	
327	4X-AXF	258C	16 Jun 78	
362	4X-AXG	258F	19 Mar 79	
418	4X-AXH	258B	21 Dec 79	

Second-hand Aircraft

Line No.	Reg'n.	Model	Delivery Date	Remarks
64	4X-AXZ	124SF	21 Jun 77	Ex-Continental N26863 and IIAF 5-291/5-8112

Leased Aircraft

Line No.	Reg'n.	Model	Delivery Date	Remarks
57	N801FT	123SF	21 Aug 77	Leased from Flying Tigers. Ret. Aug 78

QANTAS - AUSTRALIA

The Qantas 747s sported a new colour scheme, an orange cheat line and a red tail with a white winged kangaroo, when they were introduced on the Sydney-Melbourne-Singapore route in September 1971; services to London began in the November. The aircraft were also different from all previous 747s because they were the first to have the internally-extended upper deck compartment with 10 windows on each side instead of the original three. A 'lower-deck' economy-class galley was another unusual feature. Passenger accommodation at the time was for 356, with 32 in the first class who had the use of an upstairs lounge.

A 200B Combi was introduced on trans-Pacific services in 1977, and in 1979 Qantas became the first all-747 airline when its last 707s were sold. That year also saw the delivery of its first RB211-powered aircraft, which it claimed had 6 per cent better fuel consumption than its earlier JT9D-powered ones. Passenger accommodation by then had been increased to 436 on standard aircraft, and the Combis which were operated in mixed-traffic configuration had seating for a maximum of 268 passengers.

FLEET

Line No.	Reg'n.	Model	Delivery Date	Name (Prefix City of)
147	VH-EBA	238B	30 Jul 71	Canberra
149	VH-EBB	238B	14 Aug 71	Melbourne
162	VH-EBC	238B	21 Oct 71	Sydney

Line No.	Reg'n.	Model	Delivery Date	Name (Prefix City of)
171	VH-EBD	238B	8 Dec 71	Perth
195	VH-EBE	238B	10 Aug 72	Brisbane
217	VH-EBF	238B	1 Aug 73	Adelaide
233	VH-EBG	238B	19 Mar 74	Hobart
238	VH-EBH	238B	24 May 74	Newcastle
241	VH-EBI	238B	10 Oct 74	Darwin
260	VH-EBJ	238B	30 May 75	Geelong
267	VH-EBK	238B	7 Nov 75	Wollongong
285	VH-EBL	238B	29 Jun 76	Townsville
310	VH-EBM	238B	15 Aug 77	Parramatta
314	VH-ECA	238B Combi	27 Oct 77	Sale
316	VH-EBN	238B	20 Dec 77	Albury
339	VH-EBO	238B	18 Sep 78	Elizabeth
341	VH-EBP	238B	16 Oct 78	Fremantle
409	VH-ECB	238B Combi	14 Nov 79	Swan Hill
410	VH-EBQ	238B	11 Dec 79	Bunbury

SOUTH AFRICAN AIRWAYS - SOUTH AFRICA

The Flying Springbok 747s of South African Airways entered service on the Johannesburg-London route in December 1971, when they were referred to by the airline as Gentle Giants. In their coat of national colours, orange (tail), white and blue (cheat line), they soon became regular visitors to numerous European airports and through the years the 747 network was extended to Hong Kong and Sydney in the east and to Buenos Aires and New York in the west. South African was an early member of the exclusive SP Club, introducing the 747SPs alongside the 200Bs (then referred to as Super Bs) on European services in May 1976; they were later introduced on longer non-stop routes such as Johannesburg-Ilha do Sal (Cape Verde Islands)-New York and Cape Town-London.

Another name South African used to describe its 747s was Flying Hotels because of the additional facilities they had on board. In 1979, the airline was one of the few still offering its passengers the comfort of nine-abreast seating in economy-class zones, which was particularly unusual on 747SPs. The Super Bs had accommodation for a total of 343 passengers, including 32 in the first class who had the use of an upstairs lounge in flight, and the 747SPs had seats for 224 economy- and 40 first-class passengers, 16 of whom were located in the upper-deck compartment.

Current aircraft were powered by JT9D-7W engines but two 200B Combis on order were to be powered by JT9D-7Q engines. All 747s were named after South African mountain ranges.

FLEET

747-200B (Model 244B)

Line No.	Reg'n.	Delivery Date	Name
154	ZS-SAL	26 Jan 72	Tafelberg
158	ZA-SAM	13 Dec 81	Drakensberg

102

Line No.	Reg'n.	Delivery Date	Name
160	ZS-SAN	22 Oct 71	Lebombo
194	ZS-SAO	7 Aug 72	Magaliesberg
198	ZS-SAP	29 Sep 72	Swartberg
	ZS-	Due Oct 80	
	ZS-	Due Jan 81	

747SP (Model SP-44)

280	ZS-SPA	19 Mar 76	Matroosberg
282	ZS-SPB	22 Apr 76	Outeniqua
288	ZS-SPC	16 Jun 76	Maluti
293	ZS-SPD	10 Sep 76	Majuba
298	ZS-SPE	22 Nov 76	Hantam
301	ZS-SPF	31 Jan 77	Soutpansberg

TAP-AIR PORTUGAL - PORTUGAL

Operating under its original name, Transportes Aereos Portugueses, TAP introduced its first 747 on the Lisbon-New York route in March 1972. Later, as more aircraft were delivered, the 747 network was extended to Johannesburg and Lourenco Marques, via Luanda, and to Rio de Janeiro, but problems in the Portuguese possessions in Africa eventually led to a reduction in services and two aircraft were disposed of to PIA under a lease/purchase arrangement. At that time, the aircraft had seating for 372 passengers with 28 in the first class.

In 1979, TAP took on a new corporate identity and the two remaining 747s were to get a striking new red and green colour scheme.

FLEET

All 747-200B (Model 282B)

Line No.	Reg'n.	Delivery Date	Name	Remarks
178	CS-TJA	16 Feb 72	Portugal	
189	CS-TJB	16 May 72	Brasil	
239	CS-TJC	7 Jun 74	Luis de Camoes	Leased, and later sold, to PIA (AP-AYV) Apr 76
256	CS-TJD	17 Oct 75	Bartolomeu de Gusmao	Leased, and later sold, to PIA (AP-AYW) Apr 76

VIASA - VENEZUELA

A subject of much confusion and heated argument among aircraft spotters during the years 1972-74 was a 747 which had the colour scheme of one airline on one side and that of another on the other. This was KLM's 747 PH-BUG which retained its KLM colours on the left-hand side and had a VIASA colour scheme on the right-hand side, under a part lease/interchange arrangement. With its double identity, PH-BUG inaugurated a weekly Caracas-Madrid-Paris service in February 1972, to which was added later a weekly Caracas-

103

Madrid-Rome service, with some flights originating/terminating in Maracaibo and Panama. These services continued until June 1974 when DC-10s took over.

The airline's name appeared again on 747s in 1979, but only in the form of 'stickers' when Seaboard World freighters were used on some VIASA cargo services.

FLEET

747-200B (Model 206B)

Line No.	Reg'n.	Delivery Date	Name	Remarks
170	PH-BUG	Feb 72	Orinoco	Leased from KLM. Ret. Jun 74

No. 258 747-251F N616US.   (Boeing)

No. 51 747-146 JA8102.   (JAL)

No. 56 747-143 I-DEME Arturo Ferrarin. (Alitalia)

No. 57 747-123 N9662. (American)

No. 139 747-122 N4718U Thomas F. Gleed. (United)

No. 68 747-135 N77772 Patricia.   (Airline Publications & Sales)

No. 72 747-132 N9896.   (Delta)

No. 173 747-256B EC-BRQ Calderon de la Barca.   (Airline Publications & Sales)

No. 84 747-148 EI-ASI St Colmcille.   (Airline Publications & Sales)

No. 92 747-129 OO-SGA in later colour scheme. (Michel Coryn)

No. 96 747-206B PH-BUA The Mississippi in original colour scheme. (KLM)

108

No. 336 747-206B Combi PH-BUK Louis Bleriot.   (Boeing)

No. 100 747-127 N601BN.   (Braniff)

No. 405 747SP N603BN in later colour scheme. (Boeing)

No. 112 747-257B HB-IGA Geneve. (Boeing)

No. 186 747-230B D-ABYH. (Condor)

No. 330 747-237B VT-EFO Emperor Kanishka. (Boeing)

No. 272 747-258C 4X-AXD. (Boeing)

No. 149 747-238B VH-EBB City of Melbourne. (Qantas)

No. 280 747SP ZS-SPA Matroosberg. (South African)

112

No. 178 747-282B CS-TJA Portugal. (Boeing)

No. 170 747-206B PH-BUG Orinoco. (Airline Publications & Sales)

US AIR FORCE - USA

The 747s in service with the US Air Force served as Advanced Airborne Command Posts and were equipped with special command and communications equipment to suit them for this role. When first rolled out at Everett they looked like any other 747-200B, apart from their military markings, but they then went to E-Systems Inc at Greenville, Texas, to receive their special equipment and ended up with a lot of aerials and strange (classified) bumps on them. The first two were originally powered by JT9D-7W engines but were later modified to have CF6-50E engines, like the third one. These three were designated E4A, because their electronic equipment was similar to that fitted in EC-135s, but the fourth aircraft was designated E4B because it had advanced

113

No. 257 E4B 50125.   (Boeing)

electronics. Other modifications to the aircraft included an in-flight refuelling receptacle in the nose.

All aircraft were finished in anti-radiation white overall with a medium blue cheat line, light blue nose panel and black titles.

FLEET

Line No.	Reg'n.	Model	Delivery Date
202	31676	E4A	16 Jul 73
204	31677	E4A	3 Oct 73
232	40787	E4A	15 Oct 74
257	50125	E4B	4 Aug 75

WORLD AIRWAYS – USA

The first 200C (Convertible) versions of the 747 to be built were those for World Airways, an American charter operator, and the first two entered service in May 1973 on trans-Atlantic passenger charters. Passenger accommodation at the time was for a total of 461 in a ten-abreast, all-economy arrangement, with 16 in the upper deck compartment. The following winter the aircraft were used on trans-Pacific military cargo charters.

114

A third aircraft was leased to Korean on delivery in 1974, and the first two then became subject to short and long term leases to various airlines. A second-hand 100SF purchased in 1978 was also leased out.

FLEET

747-200C (Model 273C)

Line No.	Reg'n.	Delivery Date	Remarks
209	N747WA	27 Apr 73	Leased to Pan Am (N535PA) Oct 74 Due for ret. Dec 79
211	N748WA	25 May 73	Leased to Seaboard Oct 78 Due for ret. Dec 79
237	N749WA	10 Jun 74	Leased to Korean Jun 74-Mar 79 Leased to Braniff Apr 79-

Second-hand Aircraft – 747-100SF (Model 124SF)

Line No.	Reg'n.	Delivery Date	Remarks
42	N750WA	9 Feb 78	Ex-Continental (N26861) & IIAF (5-8110) Leased to FLying Tigers (N809FT) Jul 78-

KOREAN AIR LINES –REPUBLIC OF KOREA

Korean 747 operations started in a small way in May 1973 with two 200Bs on the Seoul-Tokyo-Honolulu-Los Angeles route. Cargo carrying was always a strong feature and the two aircraft were equipped with a main-deck baggage system in which passenger baggage is loaded into small containers which are stowed at the rear of Zone E, an option on all 747s (but not often used) to leave the underfloor holds clear for cargo. Passenger accommodation was for a total of 319, with 16 in the first class who had an upstairs lounge. In addition, the airline leased a 200C from World during the early years.

In 1978, Korean started its expansion by ordering two new 200Bs for 1979 delivery and leasing three ex-Lufthansa and Condor 200Bs and a 200F from Itel Air. Then in April 1979 it placed its biggest order yet, for 10 747s, comprising a mix of 200Bs 200Fs and SPs for delivery between 1980 and 1982.

The aircraft were in the national colours of red (tail), white and blue.

FLEET

Line No.	Reg'n.	Model	Delivery Date
213	HL7410	2B5B	1 May 73
215	HL7411	2B5B	12 Jul 73
363	HL7443	2B5B	23 Mar 79

Line No.	Reg'n.	Model	Delivery Date
366	HL7445	2B5B	11 Apr 79
	HL	2B5B	Due 80
	HL	2B5F	Due 80
	HL	2B5F	Due 80
	HL	2B5B	Due 81
	HL	2B5B	Due 81
	HL	2B5F	Due 81
	HL	B5SP	Due 81
	HL	B5SP	Due 81
	HL	2B5B	Due 82
	HL	2B5F	Due 82

Leased Aircraft

Line No.	Reg'n.	Model	Delivery Date	Remarks
237	N749WA	273C	12 Jun 74	Leased from World. Ret. Mar 79
132	HL7440	230B	8 Dec 78	Leased from Itel Air Ex-Lufthansa D-ABYD
168	HL7441	230F	20 Dec 78	Leased from Itel Air Ex-Lufthansa D-ABYE
186	HL7442	230B	7 Feb 79	Leased from Itel Air Ex-Condor D-ABYH
128	HL7447	230B	1 Jul 79	Leased from Itel Air Ex-Condor D-ABYF Leased to Saudia Jul 79-

WARDAIR –CANADA

The Canadian charter operator Wardair started 747 services in May 1973, mainly on trans-Atlantic passenger charters between Canada and Britain. Although the airline's headquarters were in Edmonton, flights were operated from all the principal cities in Canada and, as the fleet grew, 747 operations were extended to Amsterdam, Frankfurt, Honolulu and Barbados. The original two 100s were powered by JT9D-7 engines but the 200Bs delivered in 1978 and 1979 had CF6-50E engines. The seating in both versions is arranged for a total of 456 all-economy, with ten-abreast on the main deck and 16 passengers upstairs. In this all-economy layout, Zone A was equipped with 50 seats, being mainly triple seats along the sides and a group of five in the centre.

FLEET

747-100 (Model 1D1)

Line No.	Reg'n.	Delivery Date	Name	Remarks
123	C-FDJC	23 Apr 73	Phil Garratt	Built as Braniff N602BN
146	C-FFUN	15 Dec 74	Romeo Vachon	Ex-Continental N26864

116

747-200B (Model 211B)

Line No.	Reg'n.	Delivery Date	Name
326	C-GXRA	9 Jun 78	Herbert Hollick-Kenyon
368	C-GXRD	25 Apr 79	H.A. 'Doc' Oaks

OLYMPIC AIRWAYS – GREECE

Olympic Zeus was the name given to Olympic Airways' first 747, which was introduced on the Athens-New York route in July 1973. When the second aircraft was delivered, the 747 network was extended eastward to Singapore and Sydney. Both aircraft had an unusual seating arrangement at the time, with the main deck for 377 economy-class passengers and the upper-deck compartment for 12 first-class passengers who were provided with a small lounge, coffee bar, film screen and projector, toilet and a lift to bring meals up from the main deck.

The colour scheme on Olympic 747s is predominantly dark blue and white but enlivened by the multi-coloured Olympic rings on the tail, although these are not the same as those on the flag of the Olympic Games.

FLEET

Both 747-200B (Model 284B)

Line No.	Reg'n.	Delivery Date	Name
216	SX-OAA	21 Jun 73	Olympic Zeus
223	SX-OAB	7 Dec 73	Olympic Eagle

No. 209 747-273C N747WA.

No. 366 747-2B5B HL7445. (Boeing)

No. 326 747-211B C-GXRA Herbert Hollick-Kenyon. (Wardair)

No. 223 747-284B SX-OAB Olympic Eagle.   (Boeing)

No. 218 747-212B 9V-SIA.   (Boeing)

No. 84 747-148 HS-VGB Doi Suthep. (Aer Lingus)

No. 225 747-217B C-FCRA Empress of Japan. (CP Air)

No. 2 747-121 N747QC Mont Hoyo.   (Pan Am)

No. 242 747-245F N701SW.   (Seaboard World)

No. 46 747-123SF N800FT in early colour scheme. (Flying Tigers)

No. 406 747-249F N806FT Robert W Prescott in later colour scheme. (Boeing)

No. 304 747SP B-1862. (Boeing)

No. 262 747-2B4B Combi OD-AGH. (Boeing)

No. 8 747-131SF 5-285/5-8106 being refuelled in-flight by a KC-135 of the Imperial Iranian Air Force.
(Boeing)

No. 284 747SP YK-AHA November 16.   (Boeing)

No. 86 747-123 N905NA.   (Aviation Photo News)

No. 287 747-270C YI-AGN.   (Boeing)

No. 332 747-269B Combi 9K-ADA A1 Sabahiya.   (Boeing)

No. 337 747-2B3F F-GPAN.   (Boeing)

No. 108 747-148 G-BDPZ. (Author)

No. 338 747-2B6B Combi CN-RME. (Boeing)

No. 346 747-181B/SR JA8133. (Boeing)

No. 353 747-2B2B Combi 5R-MFT Tolom piavotana. (Boeing)

No. 354 747-2R7F LX-DCV. (Boeing)

No. 385 747-267B VR-HKG. (Boeing)

SINGAPORE AIRLINES – SINGAPORE

The Singapore Girls appeared on the 747 scene in October 1973 when SIA's first aircraft entered service on the Singapore-Tokyo route, later extending their activities to Australia and to Europe via Bangkok and Bahrain. In 1978 the aircraft were carrying a slogan 'California here we come' but the airline's DC-10s were used to inaugurate the service and the 747s took over the Singapore-Hong Kong-Honolulu-San Francisco route in August 1979. The aircraft used were the first of a roll-over order of 12 200Bs powered by JT9D-7Q engines which SIA called 'Super Bs'. As more of these aircraft were delivered, the original seven 200Bs, which had JT9D-7A engines, were to be sold.

Super Bs were arranged to accommodate 410 passengers, 28 first class and 382 economy, and the three-class cabin introduced in 1975 was continued, with full-fare economy-class passengers enjoying a larger Executive Zone. The Slumberette service for first-class passengers, which SIA had started in 1976, was also continued and there were ten of these berthable divans in the upper-deck compartment instead of only six in earlier aircraft. Externally the Super Bs remained the same in their dark blue and yellow colour scheme.

FLEET

Original 747-200B (Model 212B) with JT9D-7A Engines

Line No.	Reg'n.	Delivery Date
218	9V-SIA	31 Jul 73
219	9V-SIB	29 Aug 73
240	9V-SQC	29 Jul 74
253	9V-SQD	6 Feb 75
283	9V-SQE	30 Mar 76
309	9V-SQF	27 Jun 77
312	9V-SQG	14 Sep 77

Later 747-200B (Model 212B) with JT9D-7Q Engines

Line No.	Reg'n.	Delivery Date
387	9V-SQH	2 Aug 79
391	9V-SQI	16 Aug 79
399	9V-SQJ	25 Sep 79
401	9V-SQK	1 Oct 79
419	9V-SQL	Due 80
	9V-SQM	Due 80
	9V-SQN	Due 80
	9V-SQO	Due 80
	9V-SQP	Due 80
	9V-SQQ	Due 80
	9V-SQR	Due 81
	9V-SQS	Due 82

AIR SIAM - THAILAND

Thought at one time to be a bright star in the east, Air Siam (an independent airline of Thailand) operated various wide-bodied airliners in the mid-1970s but then vanished from the scene. It leased an Aer Lingus 747 in September 1973 and operated it for 2½ years on the Bangkok-Hong Kong-Tokyo-Honolulu route; the aircraft had seating for a total of 387 passengers, with all-economy on the main deck and eight first class upstairs. When this aircraft was returned, a KLM 747 was leased until operations ceased in January 1977.

Both aircraft were painted in the airline's medium blue and white colour scheme which featured a bird-in-flight symbol on the tail and Thai titling on the right-hand side.

FLEET

Line No.	Reg'n.	Model	Delivery Date	Name	Remarks
84	HS-VGB	148	28 Sep 73	Doi Suthep	Leased from Aer Lingus (EI-ASI) Ret. Apr 76
108	HS-VGF	148	20 Apr 75		Leased from Aer Lingus (EI-ASJ) in part c/s. Ret. May 75
156	HS-VGG	206B	16 Apr 76	Doi Suthep	Leased from KLM (PH-BUE) Ret. Jan 77

CP AIR - CANADA

With a colour scheme as eye-catching as Braniff's Big Orange, the orange and red 747s of CP Air (Canadian Pacific Air Lines) were given the general name of Super Orange when they entered service in December 1973 on the Vancouver-Tokyo-Hong Kong route. Later, the services were extended to include Toronto, Honolulu and trans-Polar to Amsterdam and Rome. The first two aircraft originally had seating for 305 passengers, including 28 in the first class who had the use of an upstairs lounge with early Canadian railroad decor. The last two aircraft were often used on charters and had increased seating for 405, including 381 economy at ten-abreast and 16 upstairs.

The upstairs lounge had gone by 1979 and all four aircraft had 24 in the first class and 2365 economy (ten-abreast) on the main deck plus either 16 or 28 economy upstairs (the last two having extra exits).

FLEET

All 747-200B (Model 217B)

Line No.	Reg'n.	Delivery Date	Name (Prefix Empress of)	Remarks
225	C-FCRA	15 Nov 73	Japan	Orig. name Asia
226	C-FCRB	3 Dec 73	Canada	
244	C-FCRD	5 Nov 74	Australia	Leased to Braniff (N620BN) Nov-Dec 78
247	C-FCRE	2 Dec 74	Italy	

AIR ZAIRE - ZAIRE

For just over a year Air Zaire leased a 747 from Pan Am and operated it on the Kinshasa-Brussels-Kinshasa and Kinshasa-Geneva-Brussels-Rome-Kinshasa routes from November 1973.

The aircraft was 747 No.2, Pan Am's N747PA *Clipper America*, with its registration changed to N747QC (QC being Air Zaire's airline designator or code) and repainted in the Air Zaire colour scheme. This scheme was based on the national colours of red, yellow and green, the cheat line was red, with yellow and green edges, the rudder green, with a yellow-edged red bar at the top, and across the fin and rudder in a red circle was a gold winged-leopard adapted from the earlier Air Congo symbol; the titles were in black and the Zaire flag was painted on the nose.

FLEET

747-100 (Model 121)

Line No.	Reg'n.	Delivery Date	Name	Remarks
2	N747QC	24 Nov 73	Mont Hoyo	Leased from Pan Am (N747PA) Ret. Mar 75

SEABOARD WORLD AIRLINES - USA

The first of Seaboard World's Containerships was introduced on the company's trans-Atlantic cargo services in August 1974; this one had JT9D-7 engines but the second and subsequent aircraft were powered by JT9D-70As and the first re-engined later. All aircraft could carry 16 passengers in the upper-deck compartment; up to 1979 these had been military personnel but Seaboard planned to offer these 'Captain's Deck' facilities to the general public on the New York-Frankfurt route. However, a proposed merger with Flying Tigers could change the plans. Some 747 capacity was leased to Saudia and VIASA in 1979, so the aircraft carried 'stickers' of one or both airlines.

FLEET

Line No.	Reg'n.	Model	Delivery Date	Remarks
242	N701SW	245F	31 Jul 74	First 200F with SCD
266	N702SW	245F	30 Apr 76	First 747 with JT9D-70A
394	N703SW	245F	6 Sep 79	
396	N704SW	245F	26 Sep 79	
	N705SW	245F	Due 80	
	N706SW	245F	Due 80	

Leased Aircraft

Line No.	Reg'n.	Model	Delivery Date	Remarks
211	N748WA	273C	1 Oct 78	Leased from World

FLYING TIGERS - USA

The Flying Tiger Line, an American trans-Pacific cargo carrier, started 747 operations in September 1974 using ex-American Airlines' passenger aircraft converted into freighters (100SFs) on its New York-Chicago-Anchorage-Tokyo-Taipei route. The aircraft were in a new colour scheme comprising an unpainted fuselage with a red and blue 'cummerbund' around it and a blue tail with a white T on a red and white disc; at the time they were given the general name of 'Freight Master'. A few years later the scheme was modified, with the T disc on the tail being replaced by white titles and the general name on the nose giving way to a sub-title 'The Airfreight Airline'. When two new 200Fs were delivered in 1979 they incorporated a further small modification by having the blue titles on the fuselage outlined in white, putting the finishing touch to a smart scheme.

During the late 1970s, Tiger International (the airline's parent company) was making every effort to secure a merger between Flying Tigers and Seaboard World so that it could expand operations into the trans-Atlantic cargo market. At the end of 1979 the approval of the Civil Aeronautics Board was still awaited, but such a merger would result in a cargo carrier of impressive size.

FLEET

747-100SF

Line No.	Reg'n.	Model	Delivery Date	Name	Remarks
46	N800FT	123SF	28 Aug 74		Ex-American N9661 Leased to Pan Am (N903PA) Jan 78-Jul 79
57	N801FT	123SF	29 Sep 74		Ex-American N9662 Leased to El Al/CAL Aug 77-Jul 78
115	N802FT	123SF	22 Jul 75		Ex-American N9671
82	N803FT	132SF	11 Feb 77		Ex-Delta N9897
155	N804FT	132SF	24 Mar 77		Ex-Delta N9899
159	N805FT	132SF	6 May 77		Ex-Delta N9900

747-200F

Line No.	Reg'n.	Model	Delivery Date	Name	Remarks
406	N806FT	249F	31 Oct 79	Robert W. Prescott	
408	N807FT	249F	11 Dec 79	Thomas Haywood	
	N808FT	249F	Due 80		
	N810FT	249F	Due 80		

Leased Aircraft

Line No.	Reg'n.	Model	Delivery Date	Name	Remarks
42	N809FT	124SF	1 Jul 78		Leased from World (N750WA) Ret. due Dec 79

MIDDLE EAST AIRLINES – LEBANON

MEA's 747 operations started with a flourish in June 1975 with two of its newly delivered 200B Combis on the Beirut-London route. The aircraft were painted in the airline's current red and white colour scheme, with the cedar of Lebanon symbol on the tail in its natural colours of green branches and brown trunk. Then trouble at home brought a series of problems leading eventually to the leasing of the aircraft to other airlines. Two went to Saudia but the third was leased for a year to Air Gabon and, on its return, made a brave reappearance in MEA colours on the Beirut-London route for a few months in 1978 before it too was leased to Saudia.

FLEET

All 747-200B Combi (Model 2B4B)

Line No.	Reg'n.	Delivery Date	Remarks
262	OD-AGH	30 May 75	Leased to Saudia Jun 77-
263	OD-AGI	20 Jun 75	Leased to Saudia Jun 77-
264	OD-AGJ	30 Aug 75	Leased to Air Gabon Jun 77-May 78 Leased to Saudia Sep 78-

TRANS MEDITERRANEAN AIRWAYS – LEBANON

Like MEA, the Lebanese cargo carrier TMA had problems with its 747 operations which were conducted during the same period. TMA started by leasing a 100SF from American in May 1975 and using it on the Beirut-Amsterdam-New York and Beirut-London routes. It was painted in the current TMA colour scheme, which was a green fuselage, with yellow titles, and a yellow tail with a green disc bearing the yellow TMA triangle and black 'moustache'. Originally it had the American registration but this was changed to a Lebanese one when the aircraft was purchased later that year. Unfortunately, it over-ran the runway at Athens in the December and was out of action until April 1976. It was then joined by a second ex-American 100SF but the two aircraft were in service for only a few months before they were sold.

FLEET

Both 747-100SF (Model 123SF)

Line No.	Reg'n.	Delivery Date	Remarks
143	OD-AGC	15 May 75	Ex-American N9676
			Sold to Pan Am (N901PA) Jun 77
136	OD-AGM	2 Jun 76	Ex-American N9675
			Sold back to American Jan 77

CHINA AIRLINES – TAIWAN

China Airlines started 747 operations in June 1975 by leasing ex-Delta aircraft from Boeing, which were painted in the national colours of red, white and blue, and using them on the Taipei-Tokyo-Los Angeles route. In 1977 it joined the exclusive SP Club, introducing the 747SP on a non-stop service between Taipei and San Francisco, then added a new Combi to its fleet in 1978 and a 200B in 1979. Seating totals were 287 in the 747SP and 411 in the Combi, both with 28 in the first class including nine in berthable seats in the upper-deck compartment.

FLEET

Standard Aircraft

Line No.	Reg'n.	Model	Delivery Date	Remarks
94	B-1860	132	16 May 75	Ex-Delta N9898. Orig. leased
322	B-1864	209B Combi	20 Apr 78	
386	B-1866	209B	31 Jul 79	
	B-	209F	Due Jul 80	
	B-	209B	Due Apr 81	
	B-	209B	Due Jul 81	

747SP

Line No.	Reg'n.	Model	Delivery Date	Remarks
304	B-1862	SPO9	6 Apr 77	
	B-	SPO9	Due Apr 80	

Leased Aircraft

Line No.	Reg'n.	Model	Delivery Date	Remarks
72	B-1868	132	15 Jun 76	Leased from Boeing (Delta N9896)
				Ret. Apr 78. To Pan Am (N902PA)

135

AEROLINEAS ARGENTINAS – ARGENTINA

Political and domestic problems delayed the start of 747 operations by Aerolineas Argentinas. An ex-Delta aircraft was painted in the airline's two-tone blue colour scheme in April 1975 but a plan to lease it from Boeing had to be dropped and 18 months passed before the first new 200B was delivered (a year late). Services started in January 1977 on the Buenos Aires-Frankfurt route with calls at Madrid and Rome or Rio de Janeiro and Paris on the way. Accommodation was provided for 350 passengers including 22 in the first class.

After operating for two years on its own, the first aircraft was joined by three more in 1979 and the 747 network was extended to include a Buenos Aires-Madrid-Paris-London route.

FLEET

Line No.	Reg'n.	Model	Delivery Date	Remarks
72	LV-LRG	132	—	Ex-Delta N9896. Plan to lease from Boeing dropped. To China (B-1868)
274	LV-LZD	287B	16 Dec 76	
349	LV-MLO	287B	13 Jan 79	
403	LV-MLP	287B	11 Oct 79	400th 747 delivered
404	LV-MLR	287B	26 Oct 79	
	LV-	287B	Due Nov 80	

IRANIAN AIR FORCE – IRAN

The Imperial Iranian Air Force (IIAF), as it was then known, purchased 12 747-100s from TWA and Continental in 1975 and they were transferred to Boeing Wichita to have the side cargo door modification and other re-work for use as transports and flight-refuelling tanker/transports. The first of these entered service in September 1975 airlifting government cargo and military equipment and spares from the United States and Europe to Iran. Only ten had the SCD modification, and the two remaining 100s and two of the 100SFs were later sold back to TWA or Boeing and the IIAF then started buying new 200Fs. In 1979, following the change of regime in Iran, the aircraft were stored at Tehran.

The colour scheme on the aircraft was a green cheat line with roundels and flags of green, white and red.

FLEET

Second-hand 747-100

Line No.	Reg'n.	Model	Delivery Date	Remarks
5	5-8101	131SF	4 Mar 75	Ex-TWA N93101. Orig. 5-280
78	5-8102	131SF	14 Mar 75	Ex-TWA N53112. Orig. 5-281

Line No.	Reg'n.	Model	Delivery Date	Remarks
80	5-8103	131SF	31 Mar 75	Ex-TWA N93113. Orig. 5-282
73	5-8104	131SF	15 Oct 75	Ex-TWA N53111. Orig. 5-283 WO Nr. Madrid 9 May 76
85	5-8105	131SF	3 Nov 75	Ex-TWA N93114. Orig. 5-284 Equipped with refuelling boom
8	5-8106	131SF	14 Nov 75	Ex-TWA N93102. Orig. 5-285
151	5-8107	131SF	14 Nov 75	Ex-TWA N93118. Orig. 5-286
9	5-8108	131SF	2 Dec 75	Ex-TWA N93103. Orig. 5-287
153	5-8109	131	15 Dec 75	Ex-TWA N93119. Orig. 5-285 Sold back to TWA Dec 76
42	5-8110	124SF	22 Sep 75	Ex-Continental N26861. Orig. 5-289. Ret. to Boeing Jan 78. To World (N750WA)
58	5-8111	124	15 Oct 75	Ex-Continental N26862. Orig. 5-290. Ret. to Boeing Sep 76 To Avianca (HK-2000)
64	5-8112	124SF	30 Oct 75	Ex-Continental N26863. Orig. 5-291. Ret. to Boeing Apr 77. To El Al (4X-AXZ)

New 200F

Line No.	Reg'n.	Model	Delivery Date
315	5-8113	2J9F	22 Dec 77
319	5-8114	2J9F	27 Feb 78
340	5-8115	2J9F	29 Sep 78
343	5-8116	2J9F	23 Oct 78
400	5-8117	2J9F	—

IRAN AIR - IRAN

The rapid expansion of Iran Air, which started 747 operations in May 1976 by introducing its first 747SP on the Tehran-London-New York route, was abruptly curtailed by the change of regime in Iran. In 1978, the 747 fleet had been increased to three SPs and two 200B Combis, with more on order, and the 747 network extended to include Frankfurt, Kuwait, Paris and Rome, with further extensions planned. By late 1979, part of the fleet had been put up for lease or sale and two new 747s, an SP and the first of four 100Bs were being operated in only part colour scheme, lacking the light blue cheat line and fin sweeps but having the legendary 'Homa' bird on the fin and black titles. The other 100Bs were cancelled.

FLEET

747SP (Model SP86)

Line No.	Reg'n.	Delivery Date	Name
275	EP-IAA	12 Mar 76	Fars
278	EP-IAB	10 May 76	Kurdistan
307	EP-IAC	27 May 77	Khuzestan
371	EP-IAD	12 Jul 79	

747-200B Combi (Model 286B)

Line No.	Reg'n.	Delivery Date	Name
291	EP-IAG	5 Oct 76	Azarabedegan
300	EP-IAH	14 Mar 77	Khorasan

747-100B (Model 186B)

Line No.	Reg'n.	Delivery Date
381	EP-IAM	2 Aug 79

SYRIANAIR – SYRIA

Syrian Arab Airlines displayed its new operating title of Syrianair when it introduced its first 747SP on the Damascus-London route in June 1976. Like Iran Air, the airline was one of the founder members of the exclusive SP Club and similarly started 747 operations with SPs. However, the aircraft were selected because their reduced capacity suited the route network rather than for very-long-range operations, and they were used alongside the airline's 727s on services to various cities in Europe and to the Gulf, Pakistan and India. A joint service to New York was operated with Alia from April 1978, but the Alia 747s were used for this service, with Syrianair operating a connecting service between Damascus and Amman. In 1979, there were plans to extend the airline's network eastward to Singapore, Bangkok and Hong Kong.

The Syrianair colour scheme was medium blue and white, with blue titles and a white bird symbol on the tail.

FLEET

Both 747SP (Model SP94)

Line No.	Reg'n.	Delivery Date	Name
284	YK-AHA	21 May 76	November 16
290	YK-AHB	16 Jul 76	Arab Solidarity

PAKISTAN INTERNATIONAL AIRLINES – PAKISTAN

PIA introduced a pleasing green, gold and white colour scheme on its first two 747s which were obtained from TAP on a lease/purchase arrangement. These were used on the Karachi-London and Karachi-New York routes from May 1976 and had seating for 370 in a mixed-class (including 32 in the first class) or 423 in an all-economy configuration.

In 1979, PIA took delivery of a new 200B Combi and used it first on Hadj flights with an all-passenger arrangement having 450 seats, including 32 in the upper-deck compartment. Afterwards it was used mainly on services to the Far East in mixed traffic configurations of either cargo in Zone E and 308 passengers or cargo in Zones D and E and 204 passengers. A second Combi was due for delivery in 1980 and both were powered by CF6-50E engines.

FLEET

Line No.	Reg'n.	Model	Delivery Date	Remarks
239	AP-AYV	282B	22 Apr 76	Ex-TAP CS-TJC
256	AP-AYW	282B	12 Apr 76	Ex-TAP CS-TJD
383	AP-BAK	240B Combi	26 Jul 79	
429	AP-BAT	240B Combi	Due Mar 80	

IRAQI AIRWAYS - IRAQ

The two 747-200Cs of Iraqi Airways, which were introduced on the Baghdad-London route in July 1976, had the airline's outstanding green and white colour scheme, in which the green appears to break over the nose like a wave, descend to a trough mid-way along the fuselage, then rise to another crest up the tail. The aircraft were also unusual in being the first of the Convertible version to be equipped with a side cargo door, and an on-board loader. This loader is an electrically-powered device stowed in Zone A which, when withdrawn, has extensible legs and serves as a transporter/lift for loading containers or pallets through the SCD or nose door openings.

By 1979 the aircraft were serving various cities in Europe and operating weekly services to Kuala Lumpur and Tokyo via Bangkok.

FLEET

Both 747-200C (Model 270C)

Line No.	Reg'n.	Delivery Date	Remarks
287	YI-AGN	24 Jun 76	First 200C with SCD
289	YI-AGO	17 Aug 76	

ALIA - JORDAN

The regal, red and gold colour scheme of The Royal Jordanian Airline, Alia, made its first appearance on 747s in April 1977, when the airline's 200B Combis were introduced on the Amman-London route. In the July, the aircraft started twice weekly services to New York (calling at Amsterdam on the outward flights) and Bangkok via Bahrain. By 1979, the New York services had been increased to four a week, with two continuing on to Houston, Texas, and the airline was planning an extension of the network to South America.

Alia Combis were powered by CF6-50E engines and had seating for 382 passengers in an all-passenger configuration or 250 passengers when equipped for mixed traffic, with 25 first-class passengers and a 15-seat upper-deck lounge in both cases.

FLEET

All 747-200B Combi (Model 2D3B)

Line No.	Reg'n.	Delivery Date	Name
296	JY-AFA	13 Apr 77	Prince Ali
297	JY-AFB	11 May 77	Princess Haya
	JY-	Due Mar 81	

NATIONAL AERONAUTICS & SPACE ADMINISTRATION – USA

The most unusual payload for a 747 is likely to go down in the history books as the space shuttle Orbiters, which were carried on top of a NASA 747 from February 1977 onwards. The aircraft was an ex-American 747-100 which had its fuselage strengthened and equipped with support struts to carry the Orbiter on its back. The re-usable Orbiter was designed to go up like a spacecraft but return to earth like an aircraft, and Orbiter *Enterprise* was taken aloft in 1977 to be air-launched for a series of tests to check its handling and landing characteristics. After the successful conclusion of these tests, the 747 was used to ferry Orbiters from landing airfield to launch site. Detachable end-plate fins were fitted to the tailplane when an Orbiter was being carried, to restore directional stability.

American's red, white and blue cheat line was retained, and a red NASA logotype and black 905 painted on the tail.

FLEET

Line No.	Reg'n.	Delivery Date	Remarks
86	N905NA	18 Jul 74	Ex-American Model 123 N9668 Cvtd to Orbiter carrier Apr-Nov 76

AVIANCA – COLOMBIA

A new wavy colour scheme, similar to that on Iraqi's 747s but in red, was given to Avianca's first 747, an ex-Continental 100 obtained from Boeing after it had been sold back by the IIAF before it had been converted to a 100SF. In Avianca service it was introduced on the Bogota-Miami, Bogota-New York and Bogota-San Juan-Madrid-Paris-Frankfurt routes in December 1976. Accommodation was provided for 345 passengers, 30 of whom were in the first class and had the use of an upstairs lounge in flight.

In 1979 the airline took delivery of a new 200B Combi, which was painted in a revised colour scheme having a red and white fin with a red 'Avianca' in full, in place of the original red fin with white 'AV'. This aircraft was generally used alongside the earlier aircraft but also operated a new Bogota-Caracas-Madrid-Rome-Zurich route and a New York service which stopped at Barranquilla en route.

FLEET

Line No.	Reg'n.	Model	Delivery Date	Name	Remarks
58	HK-2000	124	3 Dec 76	Eldorado	Ex-Continental N26862 and IIAF 5-290/5-8111
372	HK-2300	259B Combi	8 Jun 79		

SAUDIA - SAUDI ARABIA

Saudi Arabian Airlines started 747 services on the Riyadh-London route in June 1977 using two 200B Combis leased from MEA and painted in Saudia's predominantly green and white colour scheme. In 1978 it added the third MEA Combi, and in 1979 an ex-Condor 200B from Korean. Also in 1979 Saudia ordered six new 747s (100Bs and an SP), all to be powered by RB211 engines.

FLEET

Leased Aircraft

Line No.	Reg'n.	Model	Delivery Date	Remarks
262	OD-AGH	2B4B Combi	1 Jun 77	Leased from MEA
263	OD-AGI	2B4B Combi	1 Jun 77	Leased from MEA
264	OD-AGJ	2B4B Combi	17 Sep 78	Leased from MEA
128	HL-7447	230B	22 Jun 79	Leased from Korean

New Aircraft

Reg'n.	Model	Delivery Date
HZ-	168B	Due 81
HZ-	168B	Due 81
HZ-	168B	Due 81
HZ-	168B	Due 81
HZ-	168B	Due 81
HZ-	SP68	Due 81

AIR GABON - GABON

Like Saudia, Air Gabon started 747 operations with one of MEA's 200B Combis in June 1977. It was introduced on the Libreville-Paris route (via Geneva, Marseille or Nice) and was painted in the airline's new colour scheme comprising a cheat line in the national colours of green, yellow and blue, with blue titles and a green parrot on the tail.

In 1978, the MEA aircraft was returned and Air Gabon took delivery of a new 200B Combi, powered by CF6-50E engines. This was painted in the same colour scheme and carried a Gabon registration (TR-LXK) before delivery but was given a French one later.

FLEET

Leased Aircraft

Line No.	Reg'n.	Model	Delivery Date	Name	Remarks
264	OD-AGJ	2B4B Combi	1 Jun 77		Leased from MEA Ret. May 78

New Aircraft

Line No.	Reg'n.	Model	Delivery Date	Name	Remarks
324	F-ODJG	2Q2B Combi	16 Jul 78	President Leon Mba	TR-LXK before del.

SAUDI ARABIAN GOVERNMENT - SAUDI ARABIA

The most outstanding member of the exclusive SP Club, up to the end of 1979, was a 747SP ordered by the Saudi Arabian Government, reportedly for the personal use of King Khaled. Although a certain amount of mystery surrounded the production and delivery of the aircraft, the general story was that the King had been fitted with a heart pacemaker by a Cleveland, Ohio, hospital and that the aircraft was fitted out as a flying hospital to take the King to America in the event of problems, even being equipped for telemetry communications via satellite with the hospital. The 747SP was also likely to be used as a VIP aircraft, making it the largest and most expensive Biz-Jet up to that time, and was unusual in being the first 747SP with RB211 engines.

Although painted in the basic Saudia colour scheme, the aircraft lacked some of the secondary titles.

142

FLEET

747SP (Model SP68)

Line No.	Reg'n.	Delivery Date	Remarks
329	HZ-HM1	11 Jul 79	Made first flight 28 Aug 78 Left US on del. 27 Sep 79

KUWAIT AIRWAYS – KUWAIT

Kuwait Airways started 747 operations with its first two 200B Combis in August 1978 on the Kuwait-London route, calling at Cairo, Paris or Frankfurt en route. In addition, a service was operated eastward to Bombay and in 1979 there were plans to extend this service to Bangkok and Manila. Seating was provided for 380 passengers, including 32 in the first class on the main deck and eight in the upper-deck compartment.

All three aircraft were painted in the predominantly medium-blue and white colour scheme currently being used on the airline's 707s.

Kuwait was the 50th operator to purchase new or second-hand 747s from Boeing.

FLEET

All 747-200B Combi (Model 269B)

Line No.	Reg'n.	Delivery Date	Name
332	9K-ADA	28 Jul 78	Al Sabahiya
335	9K-ADB	17 Aug ,78	Al Jaberiya
359	9K-ADC	28 Feb 79	Al Mubarakiya

UTA – FRANCE

A novel application for a 747 Freighter was that of the first 200F delivered to UTA (Union de Transports Aeriens) in September 1978, which served as a 'conveyor belt' in a car assembly line. The parts for Peugeot 504 cars were made in Sochaux, France, and transferred to Lyon where they were loaded aboard the UTA 747 (enough for 120 cars at a time) for the flight to Kano, Nigeria; on arrival, the parts were transferred to a factory at Kaduna for assembly. A second 200F was delivered in 1979 and both were painted in UTA's highly-original blue and white colour scheme although, being windowless and near-doorless Freighters, they lacked the green doors which were a feature on the airline's DC-10s.

In 1979, UTA ordered two 747-200Bs for use on its passenger services between France and Africa.

FLEET

Line No.	Reg'n.	Model	Delivery Date
337	F-GPAN	2B3F	26 Sep 78
388	F-GBOX	2B3F	6 Aug 79
	F-	2B3B	Due 81
	F-	2B3B	Due 81

ROYAL AIR MAROC - MOROCCO

Royal Air Maroc's lone 747-200B Combi started operations in October 1978 on Hadj flights, the annual month-long pilgrimage which draws thousands of Moslems to Mecca. The aircraft's first service was from Rabat to Jeddah, the nearest international airport, and for this it was equipped to carry 424 passengers. The aircraft was introduced on the airline's scheduled services in December 1978 on the routes from Casablanca to New York and Montreal and from Casablanca to Paris, where Air France performed major maintenance on the aircraft. In normal passenger service, there were seats for 385 passengers, including 28 in the first class. In 1979 there were plans to extend the 747 operations to include the airline's Casablanca-Rio de Janeiro route.

The aircraft was painted in Royal Air Maroc's current red and green colour scheme.

FLEET

747-200B Combi (Model 2B6B)

Line No.	Reg'n.	Delivery Date
338	CN-RME	29 Sep 78

BRITISH CALEDONIAN AIRWAYS - BRITAIN

For three brief months during the winter of 1978-79, a 747 could be seen with a lion on its tail. This was the golden lion of British Caledonian and it was on the tail of an Aer Lingus 747 having a break from being leased to British Airways, in whose service it had become popularly known as Paddy Zulu (PZ being the last two letters of its British registration). It was leased by British Caledonian to enable the airline to fulfil its promise to introduce wide-bodied airliners on its London (Gatwick)-Houston (Texas) route from the end of October 1978, and it held the fort until the end of January 1979 when it was relieved by the airline's third DC-10 which had been late on delivery.

In British Caledonian service, Paddy Zulu had the blue tail with its golden lion, and the appropriate titles, but retained the blue cheat line it had acquired with British Airways.

FLEET

747-100 (Model 148)

Line No.	Reg'n.	Delivery Date	Remarks
108	G-BDPZ	28 Oct 78	Leased from Aer Lingus (EI-ASJ) Ret. Feb 79

ALL NIPPON AIRWAYS – JAPAN

The first new airline to start 747 operations in 1979 was All Nippon, who introduced the first of its 747SRs on high-density domestic routes out of Tokyo in the January. The aircraft were the first of a new 100B version with Short Range option, powered by CF6-45A engines, and were also the first 747s to have seats for 500 passengers (ten-abreast, all-economy, with 20 upstairs).

All Nippon's colour scheme was basically light blue and white, with an unusual blue 'spine' along the top; in a red disc on the tail was Leonardo de Vinci's design for a helicopter.

FLEET

All 747-100B/SR (Model 181B/SR)

Line No.	Reg'n.	Delivery Date
346	JA8133	21 Dec 78
351	JA8134	20 Dec 78
360	JA8135	28 Feb 79
393	JA8136	9 Oct 79
395	JA8137	5 Sep 79
420	JA8138	Due Jan 80
422	JA8139	Due Feb 80

AIR MADAGASCAR – MADAGASCAR

One of the lesser known 747 operators, Air Madagascar operated a lone 200B Combi from March 1979 onwards on its Tananarive (or Antananarivo)-Paris route, with calls at Nairobi and Marseille, or Djibouti and Rome, or Djibouti and Jeddah, on the way. It was operated in mixed traffic configuration with cargo in Zone E and seats for 281 passengers, including 24 in the first class in Zone A and 30 economy class in the upper-deck compartment. This Combi was unusual in being powered by JT9D-70A engines, with their distinctive long-chord fan cowlings.

The aircraft was painted in the national colours of red, green and white, with the red being used for the cheat line and the bird on the tail, and the green for the titles and the 'tree' on the tail; an unusual feature was that the whole of the fuselage was painted white rather than having just a white top.

FLEET

747-200B Combi (Model 2B2B)

Line No.	Reg'n.	Delivery Date	Name
353	5R-MFT	26 Jan 79	Tolom piavotana

CARGOLUX - LUXEMBOURG

Europe's largest all-cargo charter operator, Cargolux, added a 747 Freighter to its fleet in January 1979 and used it mainly on a three-times-a-week service from Luxembourg to Hong Kong; all services called in at the Gulf en route and once a week returned home via Taipei and Vienna. In its spare moments the aircraft was available for ad hoc charters so was sometimes seen elsewhere. The Cargolux 200F had nose and side cargo doors and was powered by JT9D-70A engines, like the Seaboard World 200Fs; another similarity between the aircraft was the fitting of windows and extra door to the upper-deck compartment, although Cargolux made no mention of plans to carry passengers up there.

The aircraft had an unpainted fuselage, apart from a red, white and blue cheat line and black titles, and a white tail with the company's red 'container' symbol.

FLEET

Both 747-200F (Model 2R7F)

Line No.	Reg'n.	Delivery Date	Name
354	LX-DCV	31 Jan 79	City of Luxembourg
	LX-ECV	Due Sep 80	

CATHAY PACIFIC AIRWAYS - HONG KONG

Rolls-Royce RB211s were chosen to power the 747-200Bs of Cathay Pacific, the first of which entered service on the Hong Kong-Melbourne-Sydney and Hong Kong-Taipei-Tokyo-Seoul routes in August 1979. The aircraft could carry a total of 408 passengers, including 26 in the first class in normal seats in Zone A and 12 more first class passengers in sleeper chairs in the upper-deck compartment; on short flights these sleeper chairs were used as normal seats but on the long flights between Hong Kong and Australia they were made available (for a surcharge) as sleeper chairs. An application by Cathay Pacific for a Hong Kong-London route was under discussion in late 1979.

Cathay Pacific's first 747 was painted in the airline's current green and white colour scheme with red titles.

FLEET

All 747-200B (Model 267B)

Line No.	Reg'n.	Delivery Date
385	VR-HKG	20 Jul 79
	VR-HIA	Due Apr 80
	VR-HIB	Due July 80
	VR-H	Due Dec 80

THAI AIRWAYS INTERNATIONAL – THAILAND

A fitting finale to the 747's first 10 years in service came when Thai took delivery of a 200B in November 1979. In its exotic purple, mauve and gold colour scheme, matching the Royal Orchid service it was to provide, it received a traditional Thai Buddhist blessing from His Holiness the Supreme Patriarch in Bangkok, after being led in procession by three elephants, the original jumbos.

Initial services were to Copenhagen and Paris via Kuwait and Frankfurt or Athens and Rome, with Los Angeles via Tokyo and Seattle to follow in April 1980. Seating was for 371 passengers, including 24 in the first class in 'slumberseats' and a divan-equipped lounge, and 39 business class in Zone B.

FLEET

Line No.	Reg'n.	Model	Delivery Date	Name
402	HS-TGA	2D7B	2 Nov 79	Visuthakasatriya
417	HS-TGB	2D7B	15 Dec 79	Sirisobhakya
424	HS-TGC	2D7B	Due Feb 80	Dararasmi
	HS-TGF	2D7B	Due Sep 80	
	HS-TGG	2D7B	Due Mar 81	
	HS-	2D7B	Due Mar 82	

TRANSAMERICA AIRLINES – USA

Trans International Airlines (TIA), the charter operator based in Oakland, California, changed its name to Transamerica Airlines just before it took delivery of its first 747 in December 1979, marking an extension of its operations to include scheduled services as well as charter work. The TIA green and white colour scheme had been revised earlier to incorporate a big white 'T' on the tail, indicating ownership by the Transamerica Corporation, so the change of name meant only a change of titles.

The five Transamerica 747s on order were 200Cs with nose and side cargo doors to suit them for both passenger and cargo charters. In the passenger role, they could carry up to 484 passengers (10-abreast, all-economy), including 32 in the upper-deck compartment.

FLEET

All 747-200C (Model 271C)

Line No.	Reg'n.	Delivery Date
416	N741TV	Dec 79
	N742TV	Due Mar 80
	N	Due May 81
	N	Due Apr 82
	N	Due May 82

PHILIPPINE AIRLINES – PHILIPPINES

The three 747-200Bs for Philippine Airlines (PAL) were rolled out at Everett in rapid succession during November and December 1979. They were due to be delivered in January and February 1980 for service on the airline's routes from Manila to San Francisco, via Honolulu, and Manila to Rome, Frankfurt and Amsterdam, via Bangkok and Karachi; there were also hopes of extending the network to London.

In their national colours of red, white and blue, the PAL 747s brought to 59 the number of operators who had taken delivery of new or second-hand 747s from Boeing and took to a grand total of 66 the number of operators who had flown their colours on 747s (including those who had bought their aircraft from other operators and those who had leased them in full colour scheme) during the 747's first ten years in service.

FLEET

All 747-200B (Model 2F6B)

Line No.	Reg'n.	Delivery Date
421	N741PR	21 Dec 79
423	N742PR	Due Feb 80
425	N743PR	Due Feb 80

FUTURE OPERATORS

Nearly 100 more 747s were on order at the end of the 747's first ten years in service. As indicated on the previous pages in this section, some of these were additional aircraft for existing operators but included in the order list were several new operators.

Due for roll-out in January 1980 was the first of three 747SPs ordered by the Civil Aviation Administration of China (CAAC), the national airline of the People's Republic of China, not to be confused with China Airlines of Taiwan (previously called Formosa). The plan was for these aircraft to have seating for a total of 305 passengers, including 44 in the first class, and for initial services to be from Shanghai to San Francisco (a route on which CAAC had earlier leased

No. 402 747-2D7B HS-TGA   (Boeing)

Pan Am 747SPs for some round-trip charters), although Peking could be added
to the route and the aircraft could also be used on the airline's routes to Europe.

The next new 747 operator to make an appearance on the assembly lines at
Everett was due to be Garuda Indonesian Airways, who had four 200Bs
scheduled for delivery between May and August 1980. These aircraft were to
have seating for 446 passengers, including 28 in the first class, in normal service
but when operating Hadj flights from Djakarta to Jeddah the seating was to be
increased to 546, the highest total up to that time for long-range flights.

Air Afrique, an airline based at Abidjan, Ivory Coast, but serving numerous
Central and West African countries, had a 747-200F due for delivery in
September 1980 and was likely to use it on services to Paris.

The last operator on Boeing's 747 order list at the end of 1979 (the 63rd
customer) was Cameroon Airlines, also from West Africa, who had ordered a
200B Combi for delivery in April 1981; this aircraft was also likely to be used on
services to Paris.

In addition to these orders, Boeing announced in November 1979 that it held
'unannounced acceptances' for 78 additional 747s. This term covered firm
orders that had not been announced by the customers plus orders that were
awaiting some final action such as government approval or completion of
financing arrangements. Included among those could have been Libyan Arab
Airlines, who had planned to order three 747s but had been refused by the US
government on political grounds.

149

BOEING 747 – Production List

On the following pages is a list of all the 747s built up to the end of 1979, plus the allocations for January 1980. The list is in line number order and gives details of each aircraft's identity from the date of roll-out until delivery; its delivery date and subsequent history are included in the Fleet Lists given for each operator in the 747 Operators' section.

This list also serves as a cross-reference between the constructor's number (Con. No.) of each 747 and its line number which has been used throughout this book.

Line No.	Con. No.	Model	Operator	Reg'n.	Roll-out Date	Remarks
1	20235	121	Boeing	N7470	30 Sep 68	
1969						
2	19639	121	Pan Am	N747PA	28 Feb 69	
3	19638	121	Pan Am	N732PA	16 May 69	
4	19637	121	Pan Am	N731PA	23 Apr 69	
5	19667	131	TWA	N93101	8 May 69	
6	19640	121	Pan Am	N733PA	18 May 69	
7	19641	121	Pan Am	N734PA	1 Jun 69	
8	19668	131	TWA	N93102	13 Jun 69	
9	19669	131	TWA	N93103	23 Jun 69	
10	19642	121	Pan Am	N735PA	1 Jul 69	
11	19643	121	Pan Am	N736PA	9 Jul 69	
12	19746	130	Lufthansa	D-ABYA	16 Jul 69	N1800B before del.
13	19644	121	Pan Am	N737PA	23 Jul 69	
14	19645	121	Pan Am	N738PA	30 Jul 69	
15	19646	121	Pan Am	N739PA	6 Aug 69	
16	19647	121	Pan Am	N740PA	13 Aug 69	
17	19648	121	Pan Am	N741PA	21 Aug 69	
18	19649	121	Pan Am	N742PA	28 Aug 69	
19	19749	128	Air France	F-BPVA	6 Sep 69	
20	19670	131	TWA	N93104	12 Sep 69	
21	19671	131	TWA	N93105	19 Sep 69	
22	19750	128	Air France	F-BPVB	28 Sep 69	
23	19761	136	BOAC	G-AWNA	3 Oct 69	N1799B before del.
24	19650	121	Pan Am	N743PA	10 Oct 69	
25	19651	121	Pan Am	N744PA	17 Oct 69	
26	19652	121	Pan Am	N748PA	23 Oct 69	
27	19778	151	Northwest	N601US	30 Oct 69	
28	19672	131	TWA	N93106	5 Nov 69	
29	19747	130	Lufthansa	D-ABYB	12 Nov 69	
30	19653	121	Pan Am	N749PA	18 Nov 69	
31	19725	146	JAL	JA8101	25 Nov 69	
32	19654	121	Pan Am	N750PA	8 Dec 69	
33	19655	121	Pan Am	N751PA	10 Dec 69	
34	19656	121	Pan Am	N752PA	16 Dec 69	
35	19673	131	TWA	N93107	22 Dec 69	
36	19729	143	Alitalia	I-DEMA	31 Dec 69	
1970						
37	19657	121	Pan Am	N753PA	8 Jan 70	
38	19674	131	TWA	N93108	14 Jan 70	

A 747 at cruising altitude leaving condensation trails.   (Boeing)

Line No.	Con. No.	Model	Operator	Reg'n.	Roll-out Date	Remarks
39	19751	128	Air France	F-BPVC	20 Jan 70	
40	19779	151	Northwest	N602US	26 Jan 70	
41	19762	136	BOAC	G-AWNB	30 Jan 70	
42	19733	124	Continental	N26861	4 Feb 70	
43	19675	131	TWA	N93109	10 Feb 70	
44	19748	130	Lufthansa	D-ABYC	13 Feb 70	
45	19780	151	Northwest	N603US	19 Feb 70	
46	20100	123	American	N9661	24 Feb 70	
47	19658	121	Pan Am	N754PA	2 Mar 70	
48	19763	136	BOAC	G-AWNC	5 Mar 70	
49	19659	121	Pan Am	N755PA	11 Mar 70	
50	19660	121	Pan Am	N770PA	16 Mar 70	
51	19726	146	JAL	JA8102	20 Mar 70	
52	19753	122	United	N4703U	25 Mar 70	
53	19752	128	Air France	F-BPVD	31 Mar 70	
54	19727	146	JAL	JA8103	3 Apr 70	
55	19781	151	Northwest	N604US	8 Apr 70	
56	19730	143	Alitalia	I-DEME	13 Apr 70	N1796B before del.
57	20101	123	American	N9662	16 Apr 70	
58	19734	124	Continental	N26862	21 Apr 70	
59	20102	123	American	N9663	24 Apr 70	
60	19754	122	United	N4704U	29 Apr 70	
61	19755	122	United	N4710U	4 May 70	
62	19782	151	Northwest	N605US	7 May 70	
63	19676	131	TWA	N53110	12 May 70	
64	19735	124	Continental	N26863	15 May 70	
65	20103	123	American	N9664	20 May 70	
66	19756	122	United	N4711U	25 May 70	
67	19757	122	United	N4712U	28 May 70	
68	19918	135	National	N77772	3 Jun 70	
69	20104	123	American	N9665	8 Jun 70	
70	19661	121	Pan Am	N771PA	11 Jun 70	
71	19783	151	Northwest	N606US	16 Jun 70	
72	19896	132	Delta	N9896	19 Jun 70	
73	19677	131	TWA	N53111	24 Jun 70	
74	19784	151	Northwest	N607US	29 Jun 70	
75	19785	151	Northwest	N608US	2 Jul 70	
76	19957	156	Iberia	EC-BRO	8 Jul 70	
77	20105	123	American	N9666	13 Jul 70	
78	19678	131	TWA	N53112	16 Jul 70	
79	20106	123	American	N9667	21 Jul 70	
80	20080	131	TWA	N93113	24 Jul 70	Ordered as Eastern N7401Q
81	19919	135	National	N77773	29 Jul 70	
82	19897	132	Delta	N9897	3 Aug 70	
83	19786	151	Northwest	N609US	6 Aug 70	
84	19744	148	Aer Lingus	EI-ASI	11 Aug 70	Stored until Mar 71
85	20081	131	TWA	N93114	14 Aug 70	Ordered as Eastern N7402Q
86	20107	123	American	N9668	19 Aug 70	
87	20108	123	American	N9669	24 Aug 70	
88	20356	251B	Northwest	N611US	27 Aug 70	First 747-200B
89	19875	122	United	N4713U	1 Sep 70	
90	20109	123	American	N9670	4 Sep 70	

Line No.	Con. No.	Model	Operator	Reg'n.	Roll-out Date	Remarks
91	19958	156	Iberia	EC-BRP	10 Sep 70	
92	20401	129	Sabena	OO-SGA	15 Sep 70	
93	19787	151	Northwest	N610US	18 Sep 70	
94	19898	132	Delta	N9898	23 Sep 70	
95	20402	129	Sabena	OO-SGB	28 Sep 70	
96	19922	206B	KLM	PH-BUA	4 Oct 70	
97	19876	122	United	N4714U	6 Oct 70	
98	20320	131	TWA	N93115	9 Oct 70	
99	19877	122	United	N4716U	14 Oct 70	
100	20207	127	Braniff	N601BN	19 Oct 70	
101	19878	122	United	N4717U	22 Oct 70	
102	20321	131	TWA	N53116	27 Oct 70	
103	20347	121	Pan Am	N652PA	30 Oct 70	
104	20013	133	Air Canada	CF-TOA	4 Nov 70	
105	20355	128	Air France	F-BPVE	9 Nov 70	
106	20348	121	Pan Am	N653PA	17 Nov 70	
107	19764	136	BOAC	G-AWND	17 Nov 70	
108	19745	148	Aer Lingus	EI-ASJ	20 Nov 70	
109	19765	136	BOAC	G-AWNE	25 Nov 70	
110	20349	121	Pan Am	N654PA	2 Dec 70	
111	19766	136	BOAC	G-AWNF	7 Dec 70	
112	20116	257B	Swissair	HB-IGA	10 Dec 70	
113	20322	131	TWA	N93117	15 Dec 70	
114	20120	283B	SAS	SE-DDL	18 Dec 70	
115	20323	123	American	N9671	23 Dec 70	
116	19823	246B	JAL	JA8104	30 Dec 70	
1971						
117	20350	121	Pan Am	N655PA	5 Jan 71	
118	19923	206B	KLM	PH-BUB	8 Jan 71	
119	20324	123	American	N9672	13 Jan 71	
120	19731	243B	Alitalia	I-DEMO	18 Jan 71	
121	20014	133	Air Canada	CF-TOB	21 Jan 71	
122	19824	246B	JAL	JA8105	25 Jan 71	
123	20208	127	Braniff	N602BN	29 Jan 71	Not del. Stored at Wichita until traded in, then sold to Wardair as CF-DJC
124	19959	237B	Air India	VT-EBD	3 Feb 71	
125	20325	123	American	N9673	8 Feb 71	
126	20117	257B	Swissair	HB-IGB	11 Feb 71	
127	20351	121	Pan Am	N656PA	16 Feb 71	
128	20493	230B	Condor	D-ABYF	22 Feb 71	
129	20352	121	Pan Am	N657PA	26 Feb 71	
130	19960	237B	Air India	VT-EBE	4 Mar 71	
131	20353	121	Pan Am	N658PA	10 Mar 71	Stored at Wichita for 5 years
132	20372	230B	Lufthansa	D-ABYD	16 Mar 71	
133	20326	123	American	N9674	22 Mar 71	
134	19732	243B	Alitalia	I-DEMU	26 Mar 71	
135	20357	251B	Northwest	N612US	1 Apr 71	
136	20390	123	American	N9675	7 Apr 71	
137	19825	246B	JAL	JA8106	17 Apr 71	
138	19924	206B	KLM	PH-BUC	19 Apr 71	
139	19879	122	United	N4718U	26 Apr 71	

Line No.	Con. No.	Model	Operator	Reg'n.	Roll-out Date	Remarks
140	20315	258B	El Al	4X-AXA	28 Apr 71	
141	20358	251B	Northwest	N613US	6 May 71	
142	20354	121	Pan Am	N659PA	17 May 71	Stored at Wichita for 2½ years
143	20391	123	American	N9676	18 May 71	
144	20015	133	Air Canada	CF-TOC	24 May 71	
145	19880	122	United	N4719U	28 May 71	
146	20305	124	Continental	N26864	2 Jun 71	
147	20009	238B	Qantas	VH-EBA	10 Jun 71	
148	19881	122	United	N4720U	16 Jun 71	
149	20010	238B	Qantas	VH-EBB	22 Jun 71	
150	20269	136	BOAC	G-AWNG	28 Jun 71	
151	20082	131	TWA	N93118	2 Jul 71	Ordered as Eastern N7403Q
152	20398	206B	KLM	PH-BUD	9 Jul 71	
153	20083	131	TWA	N93119	15 Jul 71	Ordered as Eastern N7404Q
154	20237	244B	SAA	ZS-SAL	21 Jul 71	N1795B before del.
155	20246	132	Delta	N9899	27 Jul 71	
156	20399	206B	KLM	PH-BUE	2 Aug 71	
157	20400	206B	KLM	PH-BUF	6 Aug 71	
158	20238	244B	SAA	ZS-SAM	12 Aug 71	
159	20247	132	Delta	N9900	18 Aug 71	
160	20239	244B	SAA	ZS-SAN	24 Aug 71	
161	20332	146	JAL	JA8107	30 Aug 71	
162	20011	238B	Qantas	VH-EBC	3 Sep 71	
163	20359	251B	Northwest	N614US	10 Sep 71	
164	20274	258B	El Al	4X-AXB	16 Sep 71	
165	20360	251B	Northwest	N615US	22 Sep 71	
166	20333	246B	JAL	JA8108	26 Sep 71	
167	20121	283B	SAS	OY-KHA	4 Oct 71	
168	20373	230F	Lufthansa	D-ABYE	14 Oct 71	First 747-200F N1794B before del.
169	20270	136	BOAC	G-AWNH	13 Oct 71	
170	20427	206B	KLM	PH-BUG	20 Oct 71	
171	20012	238B	Qantas	VH-EBD	26 Oct 71	
172	20271	136	BOAC	G-AWNI	1 Nov 71	
173	20137	256B	Iberia	EC-BRQ	4 Nov 71	
174	20376	128	Air France	F-BPVF	12 Nov 71	
175	19882	122	United	N4723U	22 Nov 71	
176	20377	128	Air France	F-BPVG	2 Dec 71	
177	20378	128	Air France	F-BPVH	10 Dec 71	
178	20501	282B	TAP	CS-TJA	20 Dec 71	
1972						
179	20527	230B	Lufthansa	D-ABYG	5 Jan 72	
180	20503	246B	JAL	JA8109	13 Jan 72	
181	20504	246B	JAL	JA8110	21 Jan 72	
182	20505	246B	JAL	JA8111	1 Feb 72	
183	20272	136	BOAC	G-AWNJ	10 Feb 72	
184	20273	136	BOAC	G-AWNK	18 Feb 72	
185	20459	237B	Air India	VT-EBN	25 Feb 72	
186	20559	230B	Condor	D-ABYH	1 Mar 72	
187	20284	136	BOAC	G-AWNL	15 Mar 72	
188	20558	237B	Air India	VT-EBO	28 Mar 72	

Line No.	Con. No.	Model	Operator	Reg'n.	Roll-out Date	Remarks
189	20502	282B	TAP	CS-TJB	11 Apr 72	
190	20520	243B	Alitalia	I-DEMB	24 Apr 72	
191	20528	146	JAL	JA8112	9 May 72	
192	20529	246B	JAL	JA8113	23 May 72	
193	19883	122	United	N4727U	7 Jun 72	
194	20556	244B	SAA	ZS-SAO	21 Jun 72	
195	20534	238B	Qantas	VH-EBE	6 Jul 72	
196	20530	246B	JAL	JA8114	20 Jul 72	N1800B before del.
197	20531	146	JAL	JA8115	2 Aug 72	
198	20557	244B	SAA	ZS-SAP	28 Aug 72	
199	20532	146	JAL	JA8116	15 Sep 72	
200	20541	128	Air France	N28903	29 Sep 72	
201	20542	128	Air France	N28888	13 Oct 72	
202	20862	E4A	USAF	31676	27 Oct 72	First Military 747
203	20543	128	Air France	N28899	10 Nov 72	
204	20683	E4A	USAF	31677	28 Nov 72	
205	19925	122	United	N4728U	12 Dec 72	
1973						
206	19926	122	United	N4729U	3 Jan 73	
207	19927	122	United	N4732U	17 Jan 73	
208	19928	122	United	N4735U	31 Jan 73	
209	20651	273C	World	N747WA	28 Feb 73	First 747-200C
210	20708	136	BOAC	G-AWNM	26 Feb 73	
211	20652	273C	World	N748WA	28 Mar 73	
212	20704	258B	El Al	4X-AXC	22 Mar 73	N1799B before del.
213	20770	2B5B	Korean	HL7410	5 Apr 73	N1798B before del.
214	20767	133	Air Canada	CF-TOD	19 Apr 73	
215	20771	2B5B	Korean	HL7411	8 May 73	N1796B before del.
216	20742	284B	Olympic	SX-OAA	17 May 73	
217	20535	238B	Qantas	VH-EBF	7 Jun 73	
218	20712	212B	SIA	9V-SIA	21 Jun 73	
219	20713	212B	SIA	9V-SIB	6 Jul 73	
220	20809	136	British A/W	G-AWNN	20 Jul 73	
221	20781	SR46	JAL	JA8117	3 Aug 73	First 747SR N1795B before del.
222	20810	136	British A/W	G-AWNO	31 Aug 73	
223	20825	284B	Olympic	SX-OAB	17 Sep 73	
224	20798	128	Air France	F-BPVL	1 Oct 73	
225	20801	217B	CP Air	C-FCRA	15 Oct 73	N1794B before del.
226	20802	217B	CP Air	C-FCRB	29 Oct 73	
227	20799	128	Air France	N63305	9 Nov 73	
228	20800	128	Air France	N28366	1 Dec 73	
229	20782	SR46	JAL	JA8118	2 Dec 73	
1974						
230	20783	SR46	JAL	JA8119	4 Jan 74	
231	20784	SR46	JAL	JA8120	18 Jan 74	
232	20684	E4A	USAF	40787	1 Feb 74	First 747 with GE engines
233	20841	238B	Qantas	VH-EBG	15 Feb 74	
234	20923	SR46	JAL	JA8121	25 Feb 74	
235	20924	246B	JAL	JA8122	8 Mar 74	
236	20881	133	Air Canada	C-FTOE	29 Mar 74	
237	20653	273C	World	N749WA	12 Apr 74	
238	20842	238B	Qantas	VH-EBH	26 Apr 74	

Line No.	Con. No.	Model	Operator	Reg'n.	Roll-out Date	Remarks
239	20928	282B	TAP	CS-TJC	8 May 74	
240	20888	212B	SIA	9V-SQC	24 May 74	
241	20921	238B	Qantas	VH-EBI	10 Jun 74	
242	20826	245F	Seaboard	N701SW	24 Jun 74	First 747-200F with SCD
243	21034	246F	JAL	JA8123	9 Jul 74	
244	20927	217B	CP Air	C-FCRD	23 Jul 74	
245	20887	228F	Air France	N18815	20 Aug 74	
246	20952	136	British A/W	G-AWNP	3 Sep 74	
247	20929	217B	CP Air	C-FCRE	18 Sep 74	
248	20953	136	British A/W	G-BBPU	2 Oct 74	Stored at Wichita for 4 months
249	21032	SR46	JAL	JA8124	16 Oct 74	
250	20977	233B Combi	Air Canada	C-GAGA	30 Oct 74	First 747-200B Combi N8297V before del.
251	21030	246B	JAL	JA8125	13 Nov 74	
252	20954	128	Air France	F-BPVP	27 Nov 74	
253	21048	212B	SIA	9V-SQD	13 Dec 74	
1975						
254	21033	SR46	JAL	JA8126	8 Jan 75	
255	21031	246B	JAL	JA8127	22 Jan 75	
256	21035	282B	TAP	CS-TJD	5 Feb 75	
257	20949	E4B	USAF	50125	19 Feb 75	
258	21120	251F	Northwest	N616US	5 Mar 75	
259	21029	146	JAL	JA8128	19 Mar 75	
260	21054	238B	Qantas	VH-EBJ	2 Apr 75	
261	21121	251F	Northwest	N617US	16 Apr 75	
262	21097	2B4B Combi	MEA	OD-AGH	30 Apr 75	
263	21098	2B4B Combi	MEA	OD-AGI	20 May 75	
264	21099	2B4B Combi	MEA	OD-AGJ	10 Jun 75	
265	21022	SP21	Pan Am	N530PA	19 May 75	First 747SP N747SP before del.
266	20827	245F	Seaboard	N702SW	24 Jun 75	
267	21140	238B	Qantas	VH-EBK	18 Jul 75	
268	21023	SP21	Pan Am	N531PA	30 Jun 75	N247SP before del.
269	21122	251F	Northwest	N618US	2 Aug 75	
270	21024	SP21	Pan Am	N532PA	3 Sep 75	N347SP before del.
271	21110	206B Combi	KLM	PH-BUH	10 Sep 75	First civil 747 with GE engines
272	21190	258C	El Al	4X-AXD	2 Oct 75	
273	21025	SP21	Pan Am	N533PA	8 Oct 75	N40135 before del.
274	21189	287B	Aerolineas Argentinas	LV-LZD	22 Oct 75	Stored for 1 year N1791B before del.
275	20998	SP86	Iran Air	EP-IAA	11 Nov 75	
276	21111	206B Combi	KLM	PH-BUI	11 Nov 75	
277	21182	237B	Air India	VT-EDU	25 Nov 75	
278	20999	SP86	Iran Air	EP-IAB	16 Dec 75	
1976						
279	21141	128	Air France	N40116	12 Jan 76	
280	21132	SP44	SAA	ZS-SPA	27 Jan 76	

Line No.	Con. No.	Model	Operator	Reg'n.	Roll-out Date	Remarks
281	21213	136	British A/W	G-BDPV	9 Feb 76	Last 747-100
282	21133	SP44	SAA	ZS-SPB	24 Feb 76	
283	21162	212B	SIA	9V-SQE	8 Mar 76	
284	21174	SP94	Syrianair	YK-AHA	23 Mar 76	
285	21237	238B	Qantas	VH-EBL	5 Apr 76	
286	21026	SP21	Pan Am	N534PA	19 Apr 76	
287	21180	270C	Iraqi	YI-AGN	3 May 76	First 747-200C with SCD
288	21134	SP44	SAA	ZS-SPC	17 May 76	
289	21181	270C	Iraqi	YI-AGO	1 Jun 76	
290	21175	SP94	Syrianair	YK-AHB	15 Jun 76	
291	21217	286B Combi	Iran Air	EP-IAG	29 Jun 76	
292	21238	236B	British A/W	G-BDXA	19 Jul 76	First 747 with R-R engs. N1790B before del.
293	21253	SP44	SAA	ZS-SPD	28 Jul 76	
294	21220	230B Combi	Lufthansa	D-ABYJ	25 Aug 76	N1786B before del.
295	21255	228F	Air France	F-BPVR	9 Sep 76	N1783B before del.
296	21251	2D3B Combi	Alia	JY-AFA	23 Sep 76	N8768V and N1239E before del.
297	21252	2D3B Combi	Alia	JY-AFB	7 Oct 76	
298	21254	SP44	SAA	ZS-SPE	21 Oct 76	
299	21221	230B Combi	Lufthansa	D-ABYK	10 Nov 76	
300	21218	286B Combi	Iran Air	EP-IAH	2 Dec 76	
301	21263	SP44	SAA	ZS-SPF	22 Dec 76	
1977						
302	21239	236B	British A/W	G-BDXB	19 Jan 77	
303	21326	228B Combi	Air France	F-BPVS	8 Feb 77	
304	21300	SPO9	China A/L	B-1862	28 Feb 77	
305	21240	236B	British A/W	G-BDXC	18 Mar 77	
306	21441	SP21	Pan Am	N536PA	7 Apr 77	
307	21093	SP86	Iran Air	EP-IAC	27 Apr 77	
308	21321	251F	Northwest	N6129US	17 May 77	
309	21316	212B	SIA	9V-SQF	7 Jun 77	
310	21352	238B	Qantas	VH-EBM	27 Jun 77	N8295V before del.
311	21381	283B Combi	SAS	LN-RNA	15 Jul 77	
312	21439	212B	SIA	9V-SQG	19 Aug 77	
313	21429	228B Combi	Air France	F-BPVT	2 Sep 77	
314	21354	238B Combi	Qantas	VH-ECA	19 Sep 77	
315	21486	2J9F	IIAF	5-8113	1 Oct 77	
316	21353	238B Combi	Qantas	VH-EBN	11 Nov 77	
317	21241	236B	British A/W	G-BDXD	12 Dec 77	N8285V before del.
1978						
318	21446	237B	Air India	VT-EFJ	12 Jan 78	
319	21487	2J9F	IIAF	5-8114	26 Jan 78	

Line No.	Con. No.	Model	Operator	Reg'n.	Roll-out Date	Remarks
320	21380	230B Combi	Lufthansa	D-ABYL	9 Feb 78	
321	21350	236B	British A/W	G-BDXE	23 Feb 78	
322	21454	209B Combi	China A/L	B-1864	9 Mar 78	
323	21351	236B	British A/W	G-BDXF	23 Mar 78	
324	21468	2Q2B Combi	Air Gabon	F-ODJG	6 Apr 78	TR-LXK and N1248E before del.
325	21547	SP21	Pan Am	N537PA	20 Apr 78	
326	21516	211B	Wardair	C-GXRA	28 Apr 78	
327	21594	258C	El Al	4X-AXF	8 May 78	
328	21536	236B	British A/W	G-BDXG	16 May 78	
329	21652	SP68	Saudi Arabian Gvmt	HZ-HM1	24 May 78	At Boeing for 1 year N1780B before del.
330	21473	237B	Air India	VT-EFO	2 Jun 78	
331	21548	SP21	Pan Am	N538PA	12 Jun 78	
332	21541	269B Combi	Kuwait	9K-ADA	20 Jun 78	
333	21537	228B Combi	Air France	N1252E	28 Jun 78	
334	21576	228F	Air France	F-BPVV	10 Jul 78	N1781B before del.
335	21542	269B Combi	Kuwait	9K-ADB	18 Jul 78	
336	21549	206B Combi	KLM	PH-BUK	26 Jul 78	
337	21515	2B3F	UTA	F-GPAN	3 Aug 78	N1780B before del.
338	21615	2B6B Combi	Royal Air Maroc	CN-RME	11 Aug 78	
339	21657	238B	Qantas	VH-EBO	21 Aug 78	
340	21507	2J9F	IIAF	5-8115	29 Aug 78	N8277V before del.
341	21658	238B	Qantas	VH-EBP	7 Sep 78	
342	21588	230B Combi	Lufthansa	D-ABYM	14 Sep 78	
343	21514	2J9F	IIAF	5-8116	21 Sep 78	N8293V before del.
344	21550	206B Combi	KLM	PH-BUL	28 Sep 78	
345	21589	230B	Lufthansa	D-ABYN	5 Oct 78	
346	21604	181B/SR	All Nippon	JA8133	12 Oct 78	N8286V before del.
347	21592	230F	Lufthansa	D-ABYO	19 Oct 78	
348	21590	230B	Lufthansa	D-ABYP	26 Oct 78	N8291V before del.
349	21725	287B	Aerolineas Argentinas	LV-MLO	2 Nov 78	N1789B before del.
350	21591	230B	Lufthansa	D-ABYQ	9 Nov 78	
351	21605	181B/SR	All Nippon	JA8134	16 Nov 78	
352	21643	230B Combi	Lufthansa	D-ABYR	27 Nov 78	
353	21614	2B2B Combi	Air Madagascar	5R-MFT	4 Dec 78	
354	21650	2R7F	Cargolux	LX-DCV	11 Dec 78	
355	21627	233B Combi	Air Canada	C-GAGB	18 Dec 78	
1979						
356	21644	230B Combi	Lufthansa	D-ABYS	3 Jan 79	

Line No.	Con. No.	Model	Operator	Reg'n.	Roll-out Date	Remarks
357	21704	251B	Northwest	N622US	10 Jan 79	
358	21575	283B Combi	SAS	SE-DFZ	17 Jan 79	
359	21543	269B Combi	Kuwait	9K-ADC	24 Jan 79	
360	21606	181B/SR	All Nippon	JA8135	30 Jan 79	
361	21678	246B	JAL	JA8129	5 Feb 79	
362	21737	258F	El Al	4X-AXG	12 Feb 79	
363	21772	2B5B	Korean	HL7443	15 Feb 79	
364	21731	228B Combi	Air France	F-BPVX	21 Feb 79	
365	21635	236B	British A/W	G-BDXH	27 Feb 79	
366	21773	2B5B	Korean	HL7445	5 Mar 79	
367	21648	SP21	Pan Am	N539PA	9 Mar 79	
368	21517	211B	Wardair	C-GXRD	15 Mar 79	
369	21659	206B Combi	KLM	PH-BUM	21 Mar 79	
370	21745	228B	Air France	F-BPVY	27 Mar 79	
371	21758	SP86	Iran Air	EP-IAD	2 Apr 79	N1800B before del.
372	21730	259B Combi	Avianca	HK-2300	6 Apr 79	
373	21649	SP21	Pan Am	N540PA	12 Apr 79	
374	21705	251B	Northwest	N623US	18 Apr 79	
375	21682	227B	Braniff	N602BN	14 Apr 79	
376	21679	246B	JAL	JA8130	30 Apr 79	
377	21706	251B	Northwest	N624US	4 May 79	
378	21707	251B	Northwest	N625US	10 May 79	
379	21708	251B	Northwest	N626US	16 May 79	
380	21680	246B	JAL	JA8131	22 May 79	
381	21759	186B	Iran Air	EP-IAM	29 May 79	First 747-100B N5537P before del.
382	21681	246F	JAL	JA8132	4 Jun 79	N1782B before del.
383	21825	240B Combi	PIA	AP-BAK	8 Jun 79	
384	21743	221F	Pan Am	N904PA	14 Jun 79	
385	21746	267B	Cathay Pacific	VR-HKG	20 Jun 79	
386	21843	209B	China A/L	B-1866	28 Jun 79	
387	21683	212B	SIA	9V-SQH	2 Jul 79	
388	21835	2B3F	UTA	F-GBOX	6 Jul 79	
389	21660	206B Combi	KLM	PH-BUN	11 Jul 79	
390	21829	237B	Air India	VT-EFU	16 Jul 79	
391	21684	212B	SIA	9V-SQI	19 Jul 79	
392	21744	221F	Pan Am	N905PA	24 Jul 79	
393	21922	181B/SR	All Nippon	JA8136	27 Jul 79	
394	21764	245F	Seaboard	N703SW	1 Aug 79	
395	21923	181B/SR	All Nippon	JA8137	6 Aug 79	
396	21841	245F	Seaboard	N704SW	9 Aug 79	
397	21848	206B	KLM	PH-BUO	14 Aug 79	
398	21787	228F	Air France	F-BPVZ	17 Aug 79	
399	21935	212B	SIA	9V-SQJ	22 Aug 79	
400	21668	2J9F	IAF	5-8117	27 Aug 79	N1288E before del.
401	21936	212B	SIA	9V-SQK	30 Aug 79	

Line No.	Con. No.	Model	Operator	Reg'n.	Roll-out Date	Remarks
402	21782	2D7B	Thai	HS-TGA	5 Sep 79	
403	21726	287B	Aerolineas Argentinas	LV-MLP	10 Sep 79	
404	21727	287B	Aerolineas Argentinas	LV-MLR	13 Sep 79	
405	21785	SP27	Braniff	N603BN	18 Sep 79	
406	21827	249F	Flying Tiger	N806FT	21 Sep 79	
407	22064	246B	JAL	JA8140	26 Sep 79	
408	21828	249F	Flying Tiger	N807FT	1 Oct 79	
409	21977	238B Combi	Qantas	VH-ECB	4 Oct 79	
410	22145	238B	Qantas	VH-EBQ	9 Oct 79	
411	22065	246B	JAL	JA8141	12 Oct 79	
412	21709	251B	Northwest	N627US	17 Oct 79	
413	21786	SP27	Braniff	N604BN	22 Oct 79	
414	21993	237B	Air India	VT-EGA	25 Oct 79	
415	21961	SP31	TWA	N58201	30 Oct 79	
416	21964	271C	Transamerica	N741TV	2 Nov 79	
417	21783	2D7B	Thai	HS-TGB	7 Nov 79	
418	22254	258B	El Al	4X-AXH	12 Nov 79	
419	21937	212B	SIA	9V-SQL	15 Nov 79	
420	21924	181B/SR	All Nippon	JA8138	20 Nov 79	
421	21832	2F6B	PAL	N741PR	27 Nov 79	
422	21925	181B/SR	All Nippon	JA8139	30 Nov 79	
423	21833	2F6B	PAL	N742PR	5 Dec 79	
424	21784	2D7B	Thai	HS-TGC	10 Dec 79	
425	21834	2F6B	PAL	N743PR	13 Dec 79	
426	22066	164B/SR	JAL	JA8142	18 Dec 79	
427	22067	146B/SR	JAL	JA8143	20 Dec 79	
1980						
428	21982	228B	Air France	F-GCBA	Jan 80	
429	22077	240B	PIA	AP-BAT	Jan 80	
430	21830	236B	British A/W	G-BDXI	Jan 80	
431	21994	237B	Air India	VT-EGB	Jan 80	
432	22063	246F	JAL	JA8144ı	Jan 80	
433	21932	SPJ6	CAAC	B-2442	Jan 80	
434	21995	237B	Air India	VT-EGC	Jan 80	